LIFT OFF

New and Selected Poems 1961–2001

Herschel Silverman

A Water Row Long Shot Joint Production

Sudbury, MA / Hoboken, NJ

First Edition
9 8 7 6 5 4 3 2
Printed in the United States of America

Cover design by Elizabeth van Itallie
Layout by Michael C. Cote

LIFT-OFF: New and Selected Poems 1961–2001
Selections from published collections and magazines

Nomad, The Krishna Poems, Nite Train, Vietnam Newsreels, Bouquet for Maggie, Getting It Together, 80 Romona, Timepiece, Fool, Humm, High on the Beats, Blue Ludes, The Hey-baby Blues, Nine DeKoonings for Marian Courtney, Poems Forged in a Forest of Words, 15 Poems for Allen Ginsberg, Scrapbook Review, Northeast #1, Long Shot, Water Row Review, Lungfull, Lucid Moon, Bluestones & Salt Hay, Talisman, Blue Beat Jacket, Butcher Block, Cerberus, Hart Mag., Nostoc, Nada, Big Scream, ZZZZYNE, Atom Mind, Penny Poemsheets, Kerouac Connections, Voices Israel, Bouillaisse, Ragged Lion, Outlaw Bible of American Poetry, Booglit, Connections, Home Planet News, Venture, Squawk, Cokefish, Moody St Irregulars, Make Room for Dada, Alpha Beat Soup, Black Swan Review, Ahnoi!, Pavan, Maine Edition, Man U Code, New Mag., X-Ray Book Company, and new previously unpublished poems.

Library of Congress Cataloging-in-Publication Data
Silverman, Herschel
    LIFT-OFF: New and Selected Poems. 1961–2001/Herschel Silverman.
       p.cm.
    ISBN 0-934953-74-0   (PBK)
    1. Beat Generation -- Poetry. I. Title
    PS 3569.I925 L54 2002
    811'.54--dc21   2002016719

Water Row Books   Long Shot Productions
P.O. Box 438   P.O. Box 6238
Sudbury, MA 01776   Hoboken, NJ 07030
www.waterrowbooks.com   www.longshot.org

Contents

Stomping For Herschel Silverman

When my Massachusetts poet-neighbor Bill Costley gener-
ously lent me his copy of Krishna Poems, published in a superb
talismanic edition by Augtwofive Press (1970), I heard, and saw,
Herschel Silverman's voice for the very first time. A North Jersey
resonant resident twang, suffused with life, lament, and love.
City bus fume blasts made appetizingly kosher and heavenly. Bill
had the edge on me in that he had actually heard Herschel read.
Nothing else quite equaled it, insisted Bill, especially given
Hersch's deceptively mild-mannered straight looks. No one in
the audience anticipated the uninhibited, propulsive, be-bop
prosody about to come their way. Midnight whelm poems,
Hudson County moans, Bayonne blues, Journal Square honks,
incantatory encomia, anti-war plaints, and trademark soulful
alliterations of being – some heavy riffing weather, indeed.

That Krishna came in midnight visits and instructed Herschel
to construct a poem, be it across a soda fountain countertop or
elsewhere, was a major inspiration to me, personally, in my
twenties. Herschel's example meant, in accessible living terms,
that poetry played – or could play – a genuine role in everyday
life. I, in fact, first met Herschel at his candy store-soda fountain,
Hersch's Bee Hive, located on Avenue A, Bayonne, New Jersey,
just across the street from the high school, where he was regarded
as an esteemed mentor by the local city kids. No doubt, at the time
Herschel was probably the only poet in America – or the world,
for that matter – with his own spinning chrome counter stools
who could proudly treat his guests to chocoholic egg-creams he
mixed himself. That, and a profound regard for contemporary
poetry – especially its North Jersey/Manhattan division – second
to none. At Hersch's Bee Hive, right beneath the Pepsi clock and
portrait of JFK, the names of the Beats (Ginsberg, Corso, Kerouac,
et al., many of them friends since the 1950s), jazz notables (John
Coltrane, Charles Mingus, Jimmy Giuffre, Art Blakey, and Dizzy
Gillespie, to cite a prominent few), and poet's poets – Ted Enslin,
especially – were uttered with the same brightening intensity,
and reverence, other people ordinarily reserve in normal conver-
sation for ballplayers, cartoon characters, television stars and
lawn mowers. Hersch's Bee Hive, in reality, radiated a kind of
third eye, hip, patriotism if you will, where dissonant howls, sax
blaps and angular Monkish grooves were as automatically
wholesome, natural and expectable as the national anthem; the

latter often electrified in Herchel's poetry by nightmare-struck apprehensions, to be sure, as unforgettably revealed in such books as *Nite Train* (Bee Hive Press). This wailing Bayonnic alchemy illuminates, I dare say, much of the frank work found within this present collection.

Reading Herschel has always been an education. There is always a line, a reference, that sends you off to the library or, nowadays especially, the internet used book search. Jim Brodey, Ray Bremser, Marguerite Harris, Bernadette Mayer – I have checked them all out in just this way. But for Herschel I never would have known to. I suspect that I am not alone here. Hersch is one of the most accomplished, and sincere, cross pollinators on the scene today. His enthusiasms are infectious; they also often contain, seed-like, important literary histories. (See Hersch's recent *Bookshelf Cowboy* for plentiful leads to the latter.)

Part of – in fact, a lot of – the fun of reading Herschel is learning about his own life's errands, big and small, his routines, his likes and dislikes. They are reminiscent in their compelling detail of, say, the still-sweet 2,000-year-old fragments from the Greek Anthology. Everything brilliantly unlikely for its ordinariness is included in the ever expanding Silverman canon – getting snockered on vermouth; vamping on painful bone spurs; and the rhythmic tickle of public transportation. As concerns the latter, Krishna or no, Hersch rides the #10 and #99S buses to make all the scenes up and down the Boulevard or across the Hudson in New York City, not to forget the Hudson-Bergen Lite Rail and tubular PATH trains. For all we know, Krishna may be driving the bus or be in the motorman's compartment. This is public transportation and shoe leather rich poetry; verily, Herschel opts for the go-anywhere shod foot (and nix to pedantic classical feet).

Speaking of buses, Herschel once told me that Carl Solomon, to whom Allen Ginsberg dedicated Howl, used to work at a small bookshop located either on one of the confusing upper levels of Port Authority Bus Station on 8th Avenue in New York City (my imperfect recollection) or across the street from it (Herschel thinks this the more likely location). At the time, I was entirely taken aback to learn that Solomon had been alive so recently – hadn't he been fatally swept away by terrible Artaudian forces long, long ago? Who would have known this fascinating ancillary figure of American literature to have been in our very midst prosaically selling books in Midtown Manhattan? Not very many, but, aye! Hersch knew, of course.

— Marshall Brooks
publisher of Arts End Books
18 December 2001

from The Krishna Poems

it's Krishna
            who visits me
with warm midnite lips
                on my forehead,
who without words
                speaks my thoughts
and desires,
            and
                suggests
                    i construct a poem
in love
        for my children—
it's Krishna
            who constructs me
with words
            at midnite,
and suggests
            to my children
the shape of
            their warm lips,
and desires
            to speak my thoughts.

      * * * * *

EVERYWHERE
            i walk
                I see Krishna –
Sometimes
        i see him broken,
                his ounces spilled
    on the gum-specked
                    sidewalk,
rain splattering
                    his poems –
    i clap –
        i cry,
for Krishna's crazy.

Krishna's in need of harmonium.
Krishna's my brother.
O sing, Krishna!
shed your Karma –

O
crazy Krishna
who turns
to
the Ganges,
and
in turning to the Hudson
turns to its mad bays.
O water ALL around you Krishna.
WATER YOUR MOTHER.
O Krishna!
SOMEWHERE
it's raining.

i hear Krishna inside Charley Mingus's strings.
i saw Krishna on the nite train
a travelling representative of the Rose.
O rise in prayer for Krishna.
Krishna's in the tunnel
under
the Hudson
singing mantras,
poking
in garbage cans,
picking at the affluent,
a battered cane
a withered leg,
gimping
from can to can.

I see Krishna
await the nite train
with
lollipop in mouth and
satchel full of
marshmallow headlines
and

a cordless phone,
                his hot-line
connected on one end to the Past
                and one end to the Future.
Krishna's the lollipop co-ordinator
                of ETERNITY.

     * * * * *

                O Krishna speaks of Love,
        that It must be broken
                into bits,
        components of warmth –
                O Krishna,
                        Godhead of turntable
        turning my mystic mind
                into syllables of prayer,
        i long for the bag of peace
                that follows your act,
            that shades the splits
                and splices –

O Krishna,
        your love exists
                in the round framework
of my mind,
        your ends joined together
are Fourth of July –

     * * * * *

i deliver Krishna
                to
                        the Democrats
        wrapped in a plastic
                baggie.
He lost his SELF-control.
                i saw him
        ride a bicycle
                last Sunday,
dressed in white,
                and

ring a set of bells
            near
Washington Sq. Park.
He had on
        the peaked cap
of a Naval Officer,
            and
the POLICE came
            to move him on.
SHAME ON KRISHNA!
he shouldn't've rung those bells
He had no icecream.

* * * * *

My scarred uncle's
            a Krishna spectre,
who burns in bed
            carelessly smoking
or pisses in vestibule
            in Waldron milk bottle,
who sells shoelaces
            in Bayonne taverns,
or in Jersey City Clendenny Avenue
            at car inspection line,
and's hard of hearing,
            gimps from an old accident,
a stainless-steel pin
            holding thigh-bone together,
and's married to good Aunt Alta
            these 53 years–
O Hare Krishna
            old whiskey man
80 year tough-guy,
            ulcerous stomach half cut out,
hypochondriac,
            Klepto,
                Star of Prohibition past,
i call your name
            Charles of London
                        born.

* * * * *

can you imagine KRISHNA
    at a pinball
      machine?
his left arm lost
    at the battle
  of Kashi-BOO-Rah,
the stump tapping
    at the flipper,
the steel ball coming
     d
      o
       w
        n
         the machine
avoiding all the bumpers,
     a blasé chick
in a red dress,
    painted on the scoreboard
watching him
    as he slaps his stump
       in dismay,
his one ear reddening
      as the ball
eludes him,
   the painted chick smiling
as she puts the "haunts"
     on him.
She has ALL Krishna's money.

* * * * *

Krishna
  visible
    in the heart of Coltrane,
Krishna kids
   bounce
    rubber
    balls
on
  dead-end streets.

Krishna girls
   wear micro-skirts
 and live
   on New York's Lower East Side.
Krishna's in the wind
    of passing
      motorbikes,
  and in their roar.
 He's in the elephant's ear.
Krishna graduates college with magna cum daily.
Krishna kids in daycamp refuse swimsuits.
Sometimes Krishna's Casper the Ghost,
 or Spooky.
Krishna demonstrates at Berkeley
  at Columbia,
    at East St. Marks Pl.
 On a Loveseat at Rutgers,
      ON
 buses, trains, and planes
  bound for nowhere,
    EVERYWHERE.
 He's on the subways.
   He MAY be in the driver's seat!

* * * * *

1968
 Krishna's clubbed
    in Chicago park
     in midst of prophecy –
He carries a bag on his shoulder,
    his mother –
His love is scrawled
    on a fallen placard –
O Gangster Glory
   of Chicago!
A Convention laid to rest –
Krishna groping
    in Daley wind tunnel –
 dark Chicago,
    dark Democracy –

Krishna cries –
        the sun detached from world fetus
    swings its retinal face
                away from the Democrats –
        NOT MUCH KENNEDY HOPE
Krishna moves on to New York,
        to school decentralization–
He rides on a storm to New England,
    lays ten foot snow
            in Maine–
    Gathers momentum for '72 –
    remembering Chicago,
    weeping for a prophecy lost –

        * * * * *

a phonograph record –
            Krishna hi-fi –
                lamentations –
He's overwhelmed by chemical rivers –
    chokes in Baltimore emphysema –
    his voice angry
            cries,
        "Shame on industry!"
    he whirls around on a plastic disc
                    shouting
        CLEAN!
Be clean
    air!
        Be Clean
        water!
Cleanliness his trombone –
    Cleanliness essential for reproduction
                    of Krishna sound–
    Spinning
        spinning Krishna
                on American turntable–
    He chants in '92
            holy, holy, holy,

holy Dupont,
        holy Ciba,
                holy Geigy,
                        holy Weyerhauser,
holy New York Stock Exchange,
                        holy American Exchange,
holy OTC,
            holy the Bear,
holy all contraceptive beings –
    harmonium, drum, sitar
                    back Krishna
                            on record –

there is the sound
                of a hand washing itself,
and there is the sound
                    of a towel –

JAZZ & THE CHANGES

for Laura

I.

ordinarily
hairy jazz
a forced
        gravelly
shout of joy
of blues
of previously
repressed
        communication
    was
the declaration
                of
my constitution,
then
    a certain coolness
    set in –
jazz was the connector
collector
scatterer of insane
visions of paranoid
stereo eyes,
somehow i imagined
liting IBM checks
with hip-bulb amendments
to a national genius,
(whatever that meant
    i was getting wild),
and in the midst of this
peculiar madness
my mind was forming its Art.

II.

jazz was COMMUNICATION
of a weird sort
probably repressions
released in a mad rant.
i was speaking to Laura
confessing
baring the leaves of my story
speaking ridiculous words
on Friday evening
cafeteria paydays,
the words
laid out in breathless lines
inversions
          running on
madly
      a line becoming paragraph,
and memories
incorporated
            of California
leathery Native Americans,
                        women,
descriptions of them
oiling train wheels,
my words used
to present,
rather, overcome
my introversions,
i remember singing
                  beef stew
                          scrambled eggs
ham steaks,
a hungry madness
that i sang to Seabees
on a slow train
headed to Shoemaker, California
during the second world war,
and i accused,
            or projected
my own panic into them
and said they were in tumult,
                        they were.

III.

i thought i knew
what jazz was all about,
the swing and human beat
the vital spark of sex
of LIFE itself
magnified by sound
transcribed
let loose to express
a soul or unity of souls,
and the changes
      the
changes making possible
the art of variation
revealing the poly character
of us human gods

IV.

so i spoke to her
about the nite,
 about the taste of the nite
about the ever lingering
virginity
      uppermost
in both our minds
and the jazz
cementing
the chandelier reflections
in each our eyes.
We went to Sinatra
who snatched
with a certain sex expression
a thousand moaning
chastities
with his Paramount weapon,
the juliettes
gyrating
      in the moment's
balcony
ungirdling
      their holiday sounds

while Benny Goodman swung
taxis
     honey
in the sunny-street
darkness
     of
New York's cupidity

V.

i spoke
about the changes
wrought on me by her
lite
and i called her
Laura Sylvania
     and lit
by thesaurus
and blackberry brandy
which warmed the words
i lapsed into a panic
of breathless lines
changing mid-line
without loss of speed
by means of alliteration and
jazz-beat
i fantasied
surmised metered shoes
and remembered challah
every Saturday
and the taste of Slivovitz
whiskey
the immediate re
     action
of myself as Van Gogh
painting my couch
     (the slip covers)
and the bad madness
of the frenzy of Self
in which i whirled around

the livingroom
glancing sideways
in a full-length mirror
which appeared in blackness
reflecting a person of worth
an anecdote out of Alfred
North Whitehead

VI.

i told her
there's no Jazz
Real Jazz
without Gut
without Love
or Zen statement
no ear
without Jazz
no Jazz without Ear,
that Jazz is the daily statement
an unincorporated
release
        of the condition of
an individual's soul
                        in relation
        to God

VII.

i took her to the Jazz Gallery
wanting her to know the sound
        of Charley Mingus's strings
the feel in public
of a man a soul
expressing with his fingers
his sensitivity
                        his chaos
and his life experience
his forming
                        consciously
with sounds

                forming an order
and conveying thru his bass
                          instrument
the essence
the message
to his listeners
                to share
with kinship
the similarities
the assonance
rhyme
        rhythm
and Alliteration of Being

VIII.

i thought of Art Blakey
a fantastic drummer
an old memory of Café Bohemia
on Barrow St. New York City
who seemed to fire a luminous squad
into steely phosphorescent
                empire shapes
giving his ALL
talking Soul
                and teaching
jazz
    to us listeners
                explaining
jazz
as the only original American Art-form,

now years later
i'm having second thoughts
on this
as the emergence
                of Pop Art
cans and labels
                Batman
and go-go

the changes or
deviations of society
have now become American Art
             and
Blakey's jazz-talk
gotten under a million skins
doesn't seem so profound
for the time being
                    anyway

IX.

i remember
in our marriage-bed
crawling
         between your
mother-legs
for warmth
             for
a multitude of inexpressible
needs
         O
how many times
did i vibrate,
did the animal sincerity
freeze my face
             in taut lust
i really wanted
to speak like Mingus's strings
but all i moaned
was
"Jack and Jill go up the hill"
in midst of copulation
later i remember
             preambles
of flutey half-note
    Monday-nite poems
        sung by Jack Micheline
                and Eli Shul

X.

some changes came
in the poems of Gregory Corso
(little-boy dictionary of Street)
a voice on the hip
    Beat literary stagecoach
to Greece
an individual
            personal
original poet
a strong link between age past
and next century
and Corso's changes
were like Dizzie Gillespie,
Dizzy
    the link between
            swing-bop
                and future
the styles similar
composed of serious knowledge
past
an artist's desire for perfection
for the natural swing of free
expression
but in control
the laughter
        and
goofing around
coming up out of
extreme seriousness
ludicrous notes   with
        words
mating them to the situation
lifting
        and
supplying impetus
    for a generation
            to wonder
and behold

XI.

changes came again
rebellious leopards
        in
the sixties
their changes
          spot rebellions
against the bop
        of
progressive jazz
        and
the toned-down cool
        of
third stream
a recharging in the gut of jazz
a Free Jazz
          atonal cut-ups
animal actions
          Ornette
Coleman
        Cecil
Taylor
        Archie Shepp
            and
Albert Ayler
John Coltrane Expression!!!
oh oh oh oh oh OH OH OH
SCREECH   BANG   ROOTS OF SOUL
        REACH OUT
naturally
        years from New Orleans
a modern change
          Art –
form of dissent
        positive
avant garde
A.G.   Allen Ginsbergian
all go
  action gobbling

                    changes
a search for new expression
one's own idiom
                    negation of Academy
man's unity in their cry
    a put-down
        of ghetto insanity
    a seeking for identity

XII.

stoned
        with Phil Lamantia
        and
Tommy Wanko
        after leaving Piero
Heliczer's party
            with a "Neal Cassady
Hipster-type"
        heard blow one nite
Cecil Taylor
        in a coffeehouse
    on
Bleecker St.
        make ANGRY   BANGING
CHAIN-GANG   PRISONER-SOUNDS
                    on piano
pounding   pounding
        the ivory keys
my own anger aroused
            my
frustrations mating his
        toward
some jazz-movement unity,
            sane
man's frenzy
    O God!
            a last frantic
appeal to each other
        a death by hard piano

unneccessary death
innovations
      the changes were new
expressions of an old death
a complete ecstasy
      of American tribal moan
and howl
   truth glimpsed
      a feel
of the last enlightenment
      which comes
  with death

XIII.

the new jazz
    gnu jazz
       a fierce love of
life
  and reality
a new sound for
      feelings expressed
    thru
a horn's discord
     a drum beating like
heart
  and piano in gut
    a
similarity to the Poet Ginsberg
    his
words loving
    celebrating
      life
the sound of Sound
      revelations
clean clear
    expressions
      thornily
mad appearance of notes
      where are

no notes
          an underscoring
                              freedom
form fitting naturally around notes
                    as
a jacket of love around a rose-heart
breath of real anger
                              howling sounds that
break thru a life encrusted in sophistry
a cut-out of extraneous fillers
                    a
no-hold final pitch
                              for free flite of Soul
that's been pricked
                              and bled
                    but's
ready for more
                    the struggle goes on

XIV.

still seeking
          angry
                    mad
                              but
blessed
        confessed
                    confused
a wordy fool
          full of nonsense
diction   airy
          fusion
                    a sketch
of poet/businessman
                    going down
to his bottom line
                    wanting to
speak out
          blow words
                    like
Kerouac jazz-notes

be Michael Carvin's
                    drumsticks
                              beat
beat beat beat heart
                    against hide
then brush tenderly
                    then whistle
                              hum
then be Hammiet Bluiett
                    speak thru
baritone sax
          in voice of God

XV.

—for Budd Johnson

changes
          always changes
America into the jazz of football
Family matures
                    1960's
                              into 70's
into 80's
          into basketball
                    and
all around were drugs
                    while jazz
off in a corner
          neglected
          and
there's rock n roll
          rocking heaven
          and
     hell
          and
               there's Fusion
                              amusing
but losing
          we go to football
                    to
rock

and finally
                    back to jazz
            a
New York Festival
                and there's
a beginning again
                        soul   feels free
soars
    swings
            lovingly
                    and
we speak to each other
                    about
Jazz and The Changes

from nite train poems

nite train
  in
    the
     mind
sweeps past the doorbell,
       past
        s
         w
          i
           n
            g
           i
            n
             g
              bluenotes –
lingers
  in the fringes –
     chugs
       and tugs
   at the Present,
      at
       the BIG beat
         of Happiness
  takes off every Now
      and Then
disappearing
   for awhile
     into a distant consciousness
  returns
    ROARING
      nervously
       in
      digestive
       tract

* * * * *

out of nite train window
     the leaves are brown
         and
           f
          a
           l
            l

   DRY INTO HAIKU
nite train rides thru the autumn sky
   an untracked cock of darkness
    MISSILE to the moon –
the moon's cockability
     is the working engine
   it walks in space
     and
      sows the sky
   and leaves behind
    a golden joy

 * * * * *

nite train takes me
    to many dark cities –
i click with its beat   beat   beat –
the MOOON follows
    the uptite sky –
no voices
   or much thats unexpected sounds
but still
   the train runs true
     and
      tries to run away from sky
  hides in MOUNtains
     would draw trees
 a
  r   ness
   o   k
   u   r
    n a
    d d
    the
       hOOts,

whistles defiance
             also joy,
                      is carried away
      with itself,
               s-l-i-c-i-n-g the nite
lolls me
        in
                                        th
                 an upper b^{er}

* * * * *

eve finds star-boy
                      on nite train –
engine flash-lite
                  ILLUMINATES
      sweeps away death-wonder
                            of coffin
                                  in baggage-car
      and just plain Herschey-bar aches –
          hurtles boy thru New Mexico
                thru
      a Deming sandstorm memory
of Indian women (Santa Fe oilers)
      and scrawny chickens

                        p
                         e
                          c
                           k
                            i
                              n
                               g
                                at
                                 o
                                  b
                                   l
                                    i
                                     v
                                      i
                                       o
                                        n

* * * * *

nite train
      going around a curve
            lined with trees
a curved train
      to Perryville
         Maryland
            to carry me away
               from my Love
a nitemare train
      bending
        the straight line
           of my mind
   O WHELM OF NITE
          TRAIN of GOING
     World War I train
maybe even 19th century train
      HOT TRAIN
     crowded serviceman train
     middle-of-nite-train
   train in which i climbed over seats
  to squeeze onto a metal baggage rack
     near the ceiling
     and lay there
      TRAIN ANGEL
watching sailors petting Waves on way to Washington
    Potomac River headquarters
   my head resting on dittybag
    full of socks, hankies
      underwear,
      galley aprons
    rolled and secured
       clothestopped –

* * * * *

   i dozed approaching Trenton
   some sailors getting ready
   to depart at Philadelphia
     i slept –
   a dream of Laura

                 the two of us making it at Coney Island
                          almost drowned in undertow –
        a voice shouting
                          Wilmington   Wilmington
        the voice in train a little later shouting
                 NEWARK   NEWARK
                          and i panicked
                 leaped off the baggage rack
                          the train moved slowly
                          and passed a sign
                                   Newark, Delaware,
                 still on its way to Perryville
                          Maryland

        * * * * *

a casual
        relationship
                aboard nite train
                        i secretly
                          strain
                                reach out
                                        and around
                                                the Other
                                                yearning
                                                        to disengage
                                                        the Love
                                                                left at home –
a ring slipped off
        in the nose
                of a tunnel
                        the bareness
                          more binding
                          than metal
                                a hoarse whistle
                                        and impending
                                                destination
                                                        re-arrange
                                                                the desire
                                                                until now
                                                                        untold –

the Lite and the Day
    as seen
from nite train
          drunkenly a Wakens
              a yearning
to be home by mid-morning
    to make love
        for 48 hours
           in the LITE
   and in the   DARKNESS –
            then
       the train hauls me back
        to Perryville,
   a Valentine Breath
        and Stain
          on my mouth –
this year
    February
      is a Lion
and there is more Darkness
          than Lite
    in a reversible act –

* * * * *

on nite train
     a flutey dream –
  images of blood
       and horror
  come at me on train –
my breath squeezes the sounds
    formed by knife and hammering nails –
     i rise out of bunk
        to SCREAM
   aghast at a soldier's story –
war-nite's worst dream yet –
  a Vietnamese bulletinboard
     TACKED with bits of MEAT !!!

O nite train go FASTER –
the Cong has found the symbol for Silence!
the village children's tongues
hung out at nite –

* * * * *

lonely inward
seated on aisle –
nite moving past train
scotta scotta scotta scotta scotta
nite hypnotic
woman next to window
sharing velveteen seat –
she
at first
wary
of my sailor suit
YET
overcome by the scottahum
b
e
n
e
her   a   legs
t
h
warms
as i droop in sleep
and
rest on her shoulder
and
slide down
a couple of inches
by
fr
act
ions
somewhere in Maryland –
she holds my head

                my lips
        and warm breath
                against her –
        both of us in sleep's pretense
                all the way
                        to
        Newark New Jersey

* * * * *

PENN station
                Penn station
nite train at bottom of s
                        t
                        e
                        e
                        p
                                stairway
is coupled noisily
                        supposed to depart
                                        s
                                        o
                                        u
                                        t
                                        h
        it lay
                on
        its track
                l-o-c-o-m-o-t-i-v-e
                                aglow
        points at tunnel
                which bores
                        under
                the Hudson –
                        i am sorry for myself
        and looking
                for the 10:45
                        a neuter train
        that unwinds me from my bride –

* * * * *

i run away in mind
              in nite train
again and again
              and again
something bugging me
              money maybe
a need to scream   to cry out
              and curse with verbs
     to release the utter   Frustration
          of a rent due
          and electric gas bill –
     the lack of tears so inhibiting
          the train carrying me
     filling with a nervous gas
              the hang-ups
          coming to a halt
              for a while
          in a bottle of Fleischman's
              and some ginger ale

* * * * *

oiled eyelids
              l
               o
                w
                 e
                  r
                   e
                    d
                              to the point
where lash meets skin
                    in the rotundas

                   n
                   o
each side of the e^{s}e
Western eyelids
              after dark
                   OPEN on Chicago

on its Sandburg sights –
                        altho
                            IMMENSITY
                        alone
can weight one's memory
                    the only sense of that
                        windy city
                            is
                        the Spice
                        of
                        hog-filled
                        forbidden
                    terminal hotdogs

* * * * *

no fee is simple –
the ticket to success
                    is the toast of integrity
slightly bent in beginning
                        and later
                            the edge of love –
burnt around
            the fee collected
                usually
                h
                 a
                  n
                   g
                    s hardening
                            in a system
            geared to an extra piece
            or subtle robbery –
        and so,
            i pay for the moments
                            of silence
            in which i write my poems
        with an absolute self-denial
                as
        any other nite train reality –
            the typed tootle
                of companionship

                    aboard the Present
                        collects
                ALL round-trip vagueries
                      tears them
                        in ha/
                          lf –

* * * * *

tho many nite trains
                    course in me
                            and i
                            in them
i am going to get off
                    at eleven
crap out
    still desirous
            for the gamble
                with words
the arrangement of 26 letters
                the shake-up
                        of mind
to make a point,
            then the Burning Forecasts
and true Confessions
                    in train
                        as it pulls in my City
from the nite,
            hangs in the nite,
                        the insane earth asleep
in dark facade of countryside –
                            i am
                            the masculine Eye
in awe of Loneliness
                    aware
                        of the wheeled vehicle
that is nite train
            GREAT   PENETRATOR
                of the CITY –
            O the whelm of SELF,
                    the secret Burning

April '75: Vietnam Newsreels 'After the Times'

I.
Cam Ranh Bay.   Picturesque.
Terror,
          panic,
trapped lives fall into the greedy pit of hell,
loot,
     die,
          lie in flies –
crack soldiers stricken with terror
                                    panic,
drop off clutched airlift plane
                              after clubbing old women,
fall into the China sea–
the fall of Da Nang,
                    Corrupted Man,
in the Spring of this year
                         approaching
our Bicentennial ,
               recalling
when Right was Might –
America waves to Saigon,
                         emotions drained –
greed,
     guilt,
          guile,
               pity,
                    shame,
                         fear,
                              hopelessness,
     ruthlessness,
sighs of relief.
red alert.
               red, red, red,
telephone dead.

II.

Greed.
American insistence upon head-thru-wall.
Corruption.
1,000,000 piasters (1200 dollars)
                                    passage
out of danger
            to Cam Ranh Bay;
some paid and were thrown overboard,
some were denied leave of ship,
                    (another million piasters).
1500 orphaned babies to fly World Airways
                                    to West Coast
            says a Mr. Daly.
Old clothes for the emperor –
Vietnam wearing blood
                    on
                    blood –
Old French exhaustions recalled.
Foreign Legions dispersed.
                    What did DeGaulle say?
Moneybags
    and jewels
        snatched up by crazed crack shock troops.
    Material for Moloch tendered meat-offering.
Wild rumors. Spread with blades of helicopter.
    Grass. Bones. Burnings. Everything left behind eventually.
        The French were right. The French were right.
        Foreign Legions leave even as Caesar's did.

III.

Saigon. Paris of the Orient.
There may be an attack,
                    maybe an attack?
An attack?
        Attack maybe?
                    Saigon?
War war war war war war war war war war

where will it end?
          On the road to Saigon?
                         Temporarily?
Saigon temporary.
          Thieu attempts to ship gold bullion to Switzerland.
I think its an old movie.
Old movies think of attack.
               Old attacks make bullions for movies.
Thieusands and Thieusands and Thieusands of refugees.
O the riceworld anguish.
               Absolute end of old lifestyle.
Beginning of red-steel unbending society.
What young girls left alive to be raped,
               and
"collaborators" shot,
          and what doom
plotted so long ago in Europe
                         tightens
around American neck.
          Our sun also rose
now smudged in smoke-sky.
South Vietnamese world rots.
Decay of System?

IV.

Sealift.
          Control folds.
Ricepeople in transit.
               Flee to Saigon,
are ordered to Cam Ranh –
kaleidoscope shipboard horrors –
Nguyen Van Panic
               President –
Americans depart as French predicted –
Starvation.
Black-market thirst comes to millionaires,
their bags of money to eat
                    if they could.

Plunder Is Congress.
Loot is Cabinet.
Greedbag is Vice President.
People Things Airplane
Ah God America Cancer Terminal

V.

Mid-20th century name for corruption.
                              Whoring.
Gold-gathering.
                  SAIGON.
Fear-sweep.
Ephemeral loot.
                  Stereo for San Francisco –
Ceramic elephants for Minneapolis –
Tarnished jewel of Orient –
Soul of Asia rotted –
                  truly fear the overpowering stench
America's turn yet to come
                              grows nearer.
THAT fear gnaws.
Offshore oilmen make haste to depart –
rig-rights be damned,
                  bodies come first.
Thieu packs his gold,
                  his southern fishskin prickles
                              with orphan-bumps.

VI.

Canned-meat orphans crash
                  strapped ten across
      human cargo in C-5A jumbo jet
"the least we can do" says President Ford

VII.

Ah 'n' General Weyand says
"South Vietnam still has the spirit
                    and capacity
capability to defeat the North Vietnamese"
Weyand's words prelude to Ford's pitch for another billion dollars.
A million refugees under control of Vietcong.
How many dead,
           maimed?
Who was on the last plane from Da Nang?
And who threw the grenade at it
                    in fit of frustration?

VIII.

Dr. Pat Smith left her hospital in Kantum.
"Vietnam was like a patient on respirator.
It was a matter of just waiting for the heartbeat to stop."
"I felt what's happening to Vietnam would have happened
                    eventually,"
                    She said.

IX.

And the Germans did their thing too.
Fucked the Vietnamese women.
Sucked cream off war economy.
Flew Lufthansa
           tears of relief flowing
        getting out with their experience
           (profits
                and been loved)
           and
their whole skins.
Farewell,
        its been good to know you –

X.

Greenville Victory a ship
Thoughts go round.
Seize opportunity
                      especially on water.
A change of course is desirable.
Vung Tan in Mekong Delta
                            rather than sitting duck
                                  on Phu Quoc.

XI.

A tired howling wind here in States.
Thieu shakes up cabinet
                    as communists close on Saigon.
$3 million dollars a day aid is absurd says Thieu,
"not near enough."
First National City
Chase Manhattan
and Bank America
                  flew out of Saigon
On Pan Am 707 jet
                  hid in darkness
the former Vietnamese employees
left as Sacrifice
                  to advancing horde of Communists.

XII.

Ah Saigon Kissinger Thieu
Weyand Ford April Sunday
icecream confection   Chiang Kai Shek   Gary Snyder
catsup airlift orphans offspring
bedsheet warriors speak
generals give ground   measures to be taken
a speech   an inquiry report to Ford
rapport with ord   raddord with fepp
clash and legal grind
with Ky   with Ky   with Key
with Kai   with Shek
ky
Green

XIII.

rockets y mas milliones
y mad
y bomb
San Clemente
y All is One
y One is dead
is death to All

XIV.

Friday morning
Americans seem improper.
Vietnamese aftermath uncertain.
Reluctance here on the North
                    and aloof,
privately,
American spy-government in Saigon.
Congress help apparent.
Nevertheless Thieu wanes.
Some American officers
                    even 5 in 67
                        flew the coup.
Barring Mr. Thieu
Weyand intends to remain American.
Power provides leverage.

XV.

Monday April 21
Thieu resigns
every man
        for himself
                    against Thieu
V.P. Tan Van Hueng
                    ailing succeeds
to give away himself
                    to BIG MINH !
old comic book character?

or cool chump?
putting head on red meat block?
BIG CHUMP
            you too a general
                            (killer)
meat-hacking butcher of Youth,
                            neutralist,
Hah! !

XVI.

April 29
Almost end of month
Mayday round the calendar-pole
                        in two days –
Rent due render unto Caesar
                        the spoils
the final climax about
        PULL-OUT   PULL-OUT
American pill-out
LARGE HEADLINES in newspaper
last American out of Nam
                        says Big Minh,
and
    he means it
as only then will Cong talk truce

    * * * * *

XVII.

its over?

Benjy

— dedicated to Ben Migdoll

O Big Bomber Benjy
three-sewer-plate-pimple-ball-puncher
King Ringalevio
Johnny Knight of the White Horse
you never let me know your sweet-singing Gershwin
until i snatched your echo
in our marble apartment hallway

ah, then, Benjy, American birdman harnessed
over Amsterdam's steel-point tulips
machine-gunned in your Dupont chute

i kick at cans and spit at cracks
riled by the silent vestibule

Willow

— for Stanley Kopcinski

it must be the willow
that weeps for me
of the song of the willow
that i hear
the song's a weep tho
a blues by Ella

it can't be Spring
the weep too much lost in snow
the willow i see
is furred from the cold
yes, i guess it is the willow
each wand an arrangement of winter
yet part of a larger design
each one of us a weep
our wool burrs muffling a song,
our cry for warmth,

it looks like more snow
the damp air cold
the sky bleak
willow rods dry
cry in the wind
the leaves' gold turn to ash
whisked south by a north wind

O willow weep for me
for pungi sticks
for bombs and mortars
for young friends in Viet Nam
for lazy-dog razored flesh
for ocean's salted memories

O willow weep for me
i'll wave
i'll wake your image
i'll weep for you
weep for you

For Dr. King

He poured his soul into death.
                              Sinned
against the Establishment, loving it so,
and took on the similar sins
                              of his brothers.
Bruised and beaten in Chicago,
knifed in Harlem,
                    and shot to death
in that motel
            Memphis,
his blood still boils in America
and shall be satisfied
                    only
in the Slum's obliteration
                    and brotherhood,
a United Generation.

FOR CHARLES OLSON

O   Hey! Olson!
Hey! Everyone here,
                    present Now
                              Thinking,
                                        speaking
                                                  of you,
naming you
          so that you're here too,
                              alive Now
you are alive,
          Olson,
                in St. Marks Church,
                              2nd Ave.
and 10th St.
          New York City,
                    Wednesday,
                              Feb. 4, 1970.
Hey!
    your Maximus word-paints
                              and pictures of Gloucester,
your Pythagorean Truth
                    of on-looker!
                              Hey!
                                    in reality
poem-images
          insights
                    involvements,
                              your turn-ons,
                                        Hey!
OLSON!
      You're the Source
                    that turned-on
                              my Depressed
                                        generation
whose poems turn on you
                    Because!
                              Hey!

your Black Mountainous viewpoint
                              always present
in your Eyes,
         your I
                  that is,
                        The Universal I
I of hurricane
         akin to God-I
                  that watches us
and names us,
              thus presents us your portrait,
and Hey!
         Olson, you're ————————

A BLUESPOEM FOR LOUIS G.

— dedicated to Edith, Allen, and Eugene

Physical body's hip structure
 vanishing into bluespoem.

Louis' malignant tumor
salved by Allen-compassion.

Is Hope romantic illusion?
Is Louis? Am I/We?

Is illusion Hope?

O Louis i sing a Bayonne Blues,
i eat your tumor
                on pumpernickel
    mayo and lettuce,
your Life sandwich –

Honey drips from heart to wound,
i sprinkle myrrh from lips of love,
i sprinkle love on old memory of you,
your speaking on telephone Bayonne to Paterson,
your passing my mail on to Allen–

O Louis, Louis,
man o' richwords, funnypuns, deep-puns,
i'd like you to be there in Paterson forever –

Let 's sing to your freedom
the last blue cool words of soul –

i salute you,
your Full life of Meaning…

For Aunt Alta On Her Death

— Eruv Pesach 4/13/76

Son Jack broken up when confronted with words
of Aunt Alta's sudden death, shocked and saddened,
sobbed and moaned and clutched his sister Elaine,
and began his wrestling with Death-Reality, questioned
Death demanding the Why the Why of her sudden departure,
questioned the Why on Eruv Pesach, the Why, our
Family Matriarch our Seder's Guest of Honor
suddenly not with us, Why the emptiness-to-be at
our Seder table, Why the awful knowledge that he (Jack)
could not speak with her anymore, or tell her to sit
the dishes would be taken care of.

So, Jack wrestled
with himself, with G-d, with Life-and-Death-questions,
knowing Aunt Alta's good deeds and Heart of Love,
wrestled with angel of Death on our livingroom floor,
rolling around in torment, seeking some solace, a logical
answer, an insight into the hard-to-accept loss.
Jack's eyes streaming tears, cheeks glistening, face
aflush, blotchy, wrestling and wrestling, attempting
acceptance but unable to accept, turning his young mind
inside out, searching in all corners as he did earlier
for Chometz just two hours before.

The Passover preparation
still going on in our house. Large white pot of soup
cooking and turkey just done, and Tzimmus not yet begun.
Aunt Alta had already made stuffed cabbage (one of her
specialties), and applesauce, as contribution to the
Seder. So, Jack wrestled and sought an answer this
Eruv Pesach, and he reasoned with G-d and finally
finally got an answer, and calmly said, "Miss her so
much, but she's found her freedom."

Pesach: Passover.
Eruv: the day prior to.
Tzimmus: a dish of flanken meat, carrots, sweet potatoes;
    also referred to as a chaotic state, a stew.
Chometz: leavened food forbidden on Passover, such as bread.

TO WHITMAN

— dedicated to John Ensslin

Painting
    sloshing words
        to Whitman
Memorial Day
    1976

what memories of bicentennial year
here
   in Union City?

East from Kennedy Boulevard
34th St. crossing Bergenline
near jewelry store
Jewish Center looms
men in black suits
broadbrimmed furtrimmed hats
Morning Star ceramic art center
poetry upstairs
       in old firehouse
how interesting

O Walt Whitman
O Whitman
Walt   plucky old male-nurse
so full of Feeling
what would you say today
so many Freedoms threatened
so many new wrinkles
a Manhattan judge taps
Bell Telephone
opens, microfilms America's mail,
and overcharges stamps

O pre-Revolutionary vibes
middle-class in economic vise

taxed taxed taxed taxed
taxed and hidden taxed
subtle government follies
and not so subtle too

nitely insomniac visions
British King Georgian
and Red Scary

Spy vs Spy
System vs System
American Gulag looms
our multinational plots
make cemetery
                of mid-east
Africa
    South America
O the midnite grass-indignities
the manipulation of middle-class
and high college tariff

America a vast plantation
of Bank America
Gasoline Sisters and Con Ed
controlling partners in energy networks

O the pulled-down shades of Lord North
and Roman Empire's nose for conquest
the old teaghosts still hovering
over Boston
Ahh Walt Whitman
don't we ever learn?

Ah Walt Whitman
Painter of word-rhythm on American page
Ah Whitman
your nation's State
the state of this union of states
what can we state of ourselves?
Where to flee?

The killer bee comes buzzing death
from South America
as does C.I.A. Chilean junta stench,
as news stories and t.v.
speak between lines
about rigging and shortages,
ah the cost of coffee!

The national human states
within the geo fragment –

O Whitman what's happened to America?
What Watergate absurdities to celebrate!
D.C. Follies
Washington macho-sadisms!

What dark knowledge dooms us all
that we are unable to yet fully say?

We struggle to speak Truth
hindered by Big Control of System.

O.K.   O.K.   Walt Whitman
how swiftly passed the years
since *Leaves of Grass*
one-hundred-twenty-one Illusions
since your first true American Lyrics
since your free-verse
anti-pentameter revolution
since your prophesying
since your dooming
since your celebration
since spouting your longlined
      rhythmic isms of America
            in this your vast developing land
since this coming-together
      conglomerate of individual states
since this bloodied adolescent country
      of bully,
            and bullied,
                  and Bull

since N.Y. Post interpretation
    of American pleasure/sin
                    anguish
since this Blake-fabled land of change/
                    no change
since the metal fire-pellets
penetrate American Throat
and bleeds out our flesh,
since Kennedy our Captain
cut down as was your Lincoln

We can't seem to emerge
from our National Shock

O Walt Whitman
what kind of mind is America
where Native people
and government
continue war at Wounded Knee?

where laid-off police barricade Brooklyn Bridge

where Manhattan's garbage piles up on sidewalk

where brother once more turns on brother
    for fix of one kind or another

where closets fill with guns
and backyard with vicious dog

and so on

O the ecology! What priority?

Happy anniversary Walt Whitman
Happy your decomposition
Happy be part of earth once more
    American poems in grave hold earth together

Walt Whitman i see you in dream
you look strangely like latterday William Everson

i hear you in New Jersey
in birdcall near
            above the Hudson
i hear your man-to-man *Leaves of Grass*
rustle in love for America

Walt Whitman i call you this Memorial Day
1976
bless us with Freedom
Compassion
Peace
    and Understanding

SOME LINES FOR MARGUERITE

— dedicated to Moses Harris

New York Mother of café rhythm,
Hip maker of such swell-wrote poetries,
sharp Mod Dame mentor of Big Apple Scene –

O photogenic Queen of T.V.'s washing-machine
    cut up and pasted in residual years –

Matriarch reconciling hot and boldrunning poets

Free-verse generation-gap girlfriend to American youth
    your compassion and hi-kindness never to be forgot –

Your life-range so extraordinary,
    wife, mother, lover to all –

your musical poem-tones heard in all verse society,
        in Le Deux Megots, Le Metro,
            in churches, cafés, University,
jazzing, blowing out poems
        East Side, West Side, all around New York,
vaulting upstate to Syracuse, Woodstock Festival
        then New England, Pennsylvania,
A Plumed Horn Trumpets your words
    thru America, up from Mexico –

O i cannot believe, adjust this poem to your passing,
    i don't quite, ah, can't believe –

You kvelled here in Dr. G's,
    (sure would've loved that word,
        means swelled up with pride, joy, satisfaction,
            a grand motherly "high" and "rush"
                thru eyes, entire being) –

i meditate, think you still here
    in this café-place where you made things "tick,"
        where you spoke your strong words
            of personal opinion –

ah, am really paranoid, your passing, am obsessed,
    this memorial reading a trick to trap me
        show me as fool
            turn my words against me
                or haul me to jail, nuthouse –

O i just can't believe
    you're not adjusting "mike"
        passing basket for contribution
            or interrupting Mumbly poet
                with plea for clarity –

REALLY   miss your rare Welsh-American toasty poems,
        your delicious bitz of conversation,
            your many hospitalities.........

                2-11-78

from Bouquet For Maggie Harris

— *1/19/78*

Three M's
a huge parking lot
corner of Chance & Death
wind whips around
up my pants –
she passes by –
what is her name?
Margaret Croydon?
Marian Courtney?
Maggie Harris?
calendar of '78
photowords
a thousand Chinese months
i check the sheet of days
take them one by one
love them all
turn to Chance
disappearing around Death's corner
O Maggie
goodbye
so long

After "A Poem" by Marguerite Harris

a poem demands
its own S P A C E

sometimes is
a TALL tale

tell-tale
with personal shape
that shapes the tone

sells Self

a poem demands
the right
to its own form

to be S P A C E D   O U T

& should never have to bargain
for its fair shape
or tone

After a "Jig For A New York Boy"

"poets and losers come to huddle
together for warmth" —M. Harris

huddling
for warmth,
poets
grown old
in New York
who lost their touch
now play back
spent words
and drink wine
in a Village café

poets stare dimly
at other poets,
together
they down their aspirations
wondering
where they had lost
whatever they thought
they had possessed

the huddled poets
the lost poets
warmth gone
wordless
lost
homeless
their stoned words
live only in mind
Memory   their home

After "The Resplendent Room"

"Soon I will come to the door
of a resplendent room;
I'll shed all tackle and gear –
take that threshold alone." — M. Harris

You've made all your deals,
crossed all your bridges,
the door to the resplendent room
opens to you –

your beauty and strength
your determination to succeed,
these were your keys –

You tore down each door,
threw it away –

You crossed each threshold
alone, and fearlessly –

You gave your time
and your possessions
to make poems come alive,
to place them in splendor
in imaginary room,
now real,
Enter,   Enter.

High In Woodstock

—for Marguerite Harris

High coming into Woodstock to read poems.

In Cal La Porto's Chevy Corvair
ecstatic chanting Haré Krishna,
tailpipe held on with wire coathanger.

High diving in motel pool.
Time divided by sunshine
and recently chanted Haré Krishna's.

High on bare legs and swimsuit body
of a fat blond mama
wishing her huge breasts
would pop out poolside.

High, yet mighty uptite
when man with two huge German shepherds
came sniffing around our room
making believe he had left behind
a tube of toothpaste the nite before.
Psyched him sniffing drugs,
the silly bastard…

High, but lonely,
ringing my family back in Bayonne.

High shopping in Woodstock windows
contemplating antiques,
the passing faces and stores
becoming familiar.

High in the FAMILY Free store
reading the bulletin walls,
"rides to Chicago"
"used camping gear"
"emergencies met with love."

High on a restaurant terrace
eating healthfood salad.
O ghost of Rodale,
and thoughts of Carlton Frederick.

High in Woodstock
wondering what Dylan and Ginsberg
are doing
and where.

High early morning
walking up Tinker Street
past old white church,
hardwares, antiques,
jewelry, and notions.
Went into drugstore for coffee.
Watched commuters
climb into New York bus.

High on self
tingling in motel shower
before donning dungaree pants
and jacket,
blue polkadot kerchief
for the poetry reading.

High on Billy Faier and Alan Edmands
smoking out back
then playing banjo and flute
while i read my poems
to a packed house,
Theatre 58.

from Nine deKooning's for Marian Courtney

1. Excavation (1950)

mystic lipstick face –
mask of old play –
racetrack ploy –
old lipstick
play on words
which face race
around canvas track –
a yacht, green auto
mobile
and oh/there
a peering eye,
whale-spying
on New York landscape
the American high way –
a looking into excavation…
i see a fish
a pussycat
a kite,
story of a whale –
and more,
the middle
and rear of an airplane
California
hear, i come!
march of wooden soldier,
a starstruck rabbit,
pin-the-tail-on-ghostly-horse
turning canine,
laughing caricature
of poodle-faced-lover,
a lone adder-faced wrench,
a high-heeled shoe,
diaper

and fish-lure bobbing,
how many images in a de Kooning?
a high seat
sitting for shoeshine –
whalepuss mirrored
in portrait by Melville –
a canopy/slick entrance to Nirvana –
freeze
froze
fresh
in ice
a rinky-dink ballerina
an old couch
potato's cushion dancing
on submarine
seen
sighted
thru slot-eye
in raided farmhouse
a shtick
in de Kooning's hand
a bookend
's –

5. Parc Rosenberg (1957)

park   oil   gloss   collection
of smearsy browns
zigzags
sweet marijuana smell
smoky
coming up/out of canvas

i am high
on
blue tattered city of nite
edge of world
1957
Willem de Kooning
80 x 70 inches dark-colored oilscrawls
scrapes in barn –
in 1957
American Bohemians lived and wrote
in small hotel, Paris,
9 Git Le Coeur,
sent their Seine words to Bayonne –
de Kooning's Parc thinks waterfall
like Great Paterson tongue
mish-mashing colors –

there's Space plugged into
the painted structure
and a line of laundry
drying in the wind
awaiting song by Dylan......

from Humm

— for Laura

How to begin
this life
a poem
to speak out
about
on
around
confess
private matters
to cast doubts
& affirmations
to be uninhibited
celebrate love
share thoughts
to act out
flites of imagination
judgments taking place
& misplaced

confirmations
rejections
sounds of music
accompany these
Lady Day
Art Blakey
John Coltrane
Gustav Mahler's
celestial exhaltations
bend
shape my moods

Change at times is Fear
Negation
it's also Hope
makes new patterns

creates illusions
turns up volume
in mind

in bed
the darkness becomes
light
lit with passion
it shapes
changes words
lives in the hushed words
awakens a kindness

because i place
a pillow
my Love
under you
because i place
my love
on a pillow
i feather my nest
i hunt love
i love the nest
on my pillow
i nest in the place
under you
i place my love
in the nest
and cover my love
with kisses
& kiss your nest
and cover it

holy
placing my Love
on top of my pillow

sometimes
i think
i lie to myself

to you
i distort
falsify
Truth

not often
and mostly
defensively
thinking
that All is Illusion
can't fully accept
the absolute Wonder of You
i feel so worthless
in Reality
in the light
of your Absolute Goodness

it matters
to stick to a bargain
with due respect
with love
entering each decision

no thing
is complete
in itself
male/female
alone only halves
the fitting together
is a unity promoting
Life
the Future

from TIMEPIECE

— for Theodore Enslin

Nothing touches humankind
                    with a ticking
                                or
unaccountability
            except Time
Its hands alive
            and sweeping
                        or
go in continuous flow
                    binding all Time
as one history in process
This land counts Time
        It runs out
                    FISH   WATER   BROKEN GLASS
                        strength diminished
                                danger of extinction
                        prognosis of doom a Poet says
                            Simple bones lie in retrieval
                            Oil
                                        haunts dust
                        Energies disturbed in Time

    * * * * *
Going West is a turning
            back
            in Time
    a sliding
            altho
going far enough
the wondrous wheel comes full circle
Climbing is another story
            a caution
Tumbling rocks begin a danger
        This will be an end of Time
                    itself

All is Temporary
    Illusion bears actual fruit

dreams sorted
d i s t o r t e d
bear down
            and out
     this nite
            in Time

     * * * * *

Our feet
        feats
meet in Time
Measure
carry complaints / tread
     singly
          one
     after the other

Time is alone
     Is something else
          Another thing

     Still   high
          Clouds shout
               and
          lower the distance

     Again they all try
               never
                    get to home
                              base

From a distance
               Time immemorial
seems numb
               with a morning chill
pinched in mind
                    entranced
silent   rising
          a memorial

* * * * *

A gentle break fast
   Who lights morning
Motion of light
   comes over nite
      silent
as a feather or cloud in flight

Sweep
 Time treads water
    each
      morning
Who grooves in the motion

There is no darkness
    only area
sans light
  within eye

Light going thru dark
  becomes gladness
Here are dark poems
There is no light part of the Time

Footprints in bed testify
Footsteps in books define fake history
Fake footprints are alluring
Camels horses tanks planes
and the wheel become history in Time
   As does hair

* * * * *

We left words among the trees
Symbols
Chiselled
Painted with inks
Wrote-out our feelings
Felt wordy...bungled
Blinked in universe
Dealt failure from a deck of jokers
There's little chance of winning

or choice of another beginning
We came out of a desert & return there

* * * * *

Time crosses
        erases
            covers
itself
   with
      past performance
looking over shoulder
   it shudders in salt
Utter bewilderment
Where were we at
        up to
Where to go
Is there a plan
      Just

* * * * *

It's true
     aged joints slow
Time and again
        and again some time
times gains the upper hand
          in time
joints do slow
     slowly regain
a strength
    but slow again and again
and rebellion against time
        fails
it bends
    while healing
but as systems break down
        again
and again
    slowly
      but surely
by degrees
    into new categories

* * * * *

Time as a manuscript?
Legible.
      Illegible?
    Haphazard!
Planned.
      Plain.
        In.
A grain of rice is said.
Exact beginning?
         NO.
     End?
      NO.
Shape or sound?
    Meaning?
       Eternal?
    No one knows.

* * * * *

All is one in Time?
It Time contains All.
Everything.
     Present and Past.
Future.
   It all happens.
Concrete.
   Surreal.
     Unreal.
Real.
   Imagined.
    Possible.
Impossible.

* * * * *

Stop Time Huxley said.
Things must? at times? be measured?
Waltham Seiko Bulova Westclox
Benrus Times Swiss bejewelled
     face of
       hands of

mechanical
     electrical
          numeral
digital
  Big
    Little Big
alarm
  wrist
    pocket
      commercial
a touch of
    step in
      daylite saving
Greenwich
    East West Central
ticks and tocks
      drug alternatives
Hebrew
  Roman
    sun
      moon
        hour
minute
  second
    shadow
      noon
        mean
A D B C
    Genesis
      lifetime
        day
          week
month
  year
    decade
      century
        millennium
          specks in
            nick of
              TIME

FOOL

— for Allen Ginsberg, penpal

"Sometimes naked, sometimes mad
now as a scholar, now as a fool
thus they appear on earth –
The free men!"
— A Hindu verse

I
Free, blessed, saintly…
painting image of myself
                    flesh-face
flash of recognition
smears, drips of black
                    ink
depiction of Poet
                    mad
an April Zen Fool,
                    twisting
new meaning from tired words.
Poet gone insane
in last Sound search for
misplaced consonants,
missing vowels that fouled up
from coast to coast.

III
Free? blessed, saintly…
hid behind candycounter
from Zen to now,
to feed the hungry teenage mouths
to hug those bereaved
to give succor to
the kids kicked out of
their tv couchworld,
to feed the blind some magic sights,
and to give the athlete
a Defense for breakfast.
To startle writers
cramped by their own Illusions.

V

Free? Blessed?
Culture-freak hypnotized by movement
Duchamp's nude descending staircase.
I am a fool
       looking
in wonder
at de Kooning's ugly Women.
Empathize
       feel brotherly
for van Gogh,
O to share the perfection
of his madness.
         To share
my old fool poems
with Ginsberg, Corso,
whose own poems
for crying out loud.
To imitate Beat & Hip.
To want to be Public
a Fool of Poetry.

VI

Saintly, Blessed, Fool,
cracked
    finely hashed
fooling around in Amsterdam
in melkweg multi-media centrum
bathed in smoke
         letting go
floating
    thru Liedesplein
passing hotels restaurants
a theatre of Chagall
         hysterical
laughing in freedom
removing shoes.

VII

Saintly paranoia…
A fake poet
      a clown
in a global village
video trickery
          CIA
agent provocateurs
    wine-ply grass
offerings
      cameras
eyes on me
    secret ears
    listening
i cared
    i didn't
high on wine
        mad
loving the world
    later hugging kissing
d a n c i n g
      in the street

VIII

Free, guest of New Jersey
State Council of the Arts
a Poetry Fool awardee
1980-1981
      dancin'
reelin'
feelin' no pain
celebrating at Morven mansion
gin and tonics
a tacky jazz band
playin' PAT tunes
         soul
lost
    a-Mazed
pleasing the Princeton Establishment
    what did i do

to
deserve this?
    where did i check
             my soul
deposit in the Commercial Trust
O swing it like
             Benny
    God man!

IX
FREE
    &
      SAINTLY
BLESSED PIGTAIL POET
    Peter Orlovsky
      ZENS me

    T I C K L E S

X
I'll try to be
    a fool of Williams

Allen Ginsberg says,
    "I still think the Jersey path
      for Poetry is Williams'
        descriptive simplicity."

So, is Ted Enslin like Joe Dimaggio?
    Their acts simple.
        Appearing.
But, underneath,
          fluid,
    & a great complexity.

Many insights.
A ballplayer, a poet, a fool,
    thus they appear on earth.
        Catholic, Protestant, Jew.
          Free men?

XIX
Fool thoughts.
A going back.
East Village memory
                of runaways,
Peace march
                flowers.
Visions of Love
                and suicide.
Long hair and short skirts.
Street people and street theatre.
Panhandlers.
Rock in Tompkins Park.
Innocent expressions of Freedom.

XXI
Blessed with dada hope.
Sometimes incomprehensible.
Mystic.
A Jester scribbling his Sensitive song
beating ironic pentameter
                over head
with continuous attic convulsion.
Overheard,
        endless implications
    of verse Simplicity.
I cut up and buried
pre-Beat Hoky Notion
of BIG POEM
                in Jersey desperation.
Longed for Blessed designation,
        rejected, floundered,
                word overdosed, meaningless,
Horse-play on page.
Confusion.
Wrote with tale hung between clown-legs.

XXIII

Blessed with naked feelings,
full of love
    and
seeking love,
        at times
felt unloved,
           afraid
to communicate
            to tell it
like it is,
       it isn't easy
to shout CHEMICALS! CHEMICALS!
and go on selling Drakes cakes,
to act an eco-fool,
         protest war
yet seek security
         foolishly.
There's no answer.
Only Love.

XXVII

Saintly? Mad...
I am passing out right now,
a Vermouth Fool, drunk.
It took all these years
to face my foolishness,
my fool's face,
fool's desire to write this down
to list my foolishness.
        My Foolery.

XXIX

Mad, blessed,
        saintly?
I must be kidding, foolin' myself.
Look in mirror, see a fool
           am not fooled.

Go on writing
              spin
                    illusions
real/surreal.
      A
little different i hope.
Meshuggenah.
O could be i want to speak
                    like
Louis Armstrong,
              Lady Day,
Prez & Diz, Cecil Taylor,
that Jazz is my fool's cement.
Could be this Fool
is just a Poet
         clowning around.

San Andreas Shake-out

— for Linda Barrett

BOOM BOOM BOOM BOOM BOOM
Incomprehensible heart-hammer.
Mother-earth's thunderous stammer.
A rocking n rolling a primal acidulous adrenalin taste.
Arteries gone cold throat clammed up!
Brain pounds into bottle of bitter aspirin.
Helpless bodies buried under Bay Bridge highway!
Pacific kelpy strange sea-salt taste of hell!
Sound of giant empty dumpster dropped ten miles
reverberating bopping brain!
Textured earth like dry layer-cake crumbling
into eternal realignment!
Shocking surrealistic earth-yawn like Daliesque dessert
Earth color mish-mosh like Tex-Mex hot-pepper conniption!
Over-baked earth-potato pops its juices in West Coast Happening!
World-mind shocked into TV media event security surrender.
Bombed-out fiery rubbled marina!
Whose fault is it?

BOOM BOOM BOOM BOOM BOOM

Meditation With Memory

— for Bernadette Mayer

main thing is begin with a white sunk feeling/ in a white house/
a white horse smoking/be vivid and whispy/whispery/set
 situation
a white road to somewhere/something/maybe temptations/
 aromatic
buzzes/views of new language/understandings/transparent
 glimpses into
eternity/then type it/tape it onto page in personal picturebook/
 storybook it/something about hunger/something solid/
 something to stomach/symbols/ideas in things/saintly
 names/self-portraits in
dream-mind/all that takes place in a hot July day/at best a
 remembrance of bed-
flame/sweet jazz-cooked images/images of images/polaroiding/
 35mms/
dizziness/brite emanations/Latin textures/birds of transportation/
 herds
of automobile images that jump fences/a park in city covered up
 to neck
in noise and carbon monoxide/yellow cab-bent notes/motes of
 dusty out-
rage/a whole circus of half-finished dreams/tears/lies/cars going
 off
cliff flunking inspection/city clocks/cocks of mourning/pisces/
 eyes of
cold meat & wind-bursts/wind-ups/pieces on hot-handed
 womanizers/cages
of women on 42nd St. let out/going on Columbus journeys/
 yearnings of
headlites/headlines/collaradoes of experimental writing/bonded
 hands
banded with love/violences/bookshelves filled with chicken
 livers/
lovers infinite/fluttering alcoholics/flittering lizards/laps full of
 skewered morality/
chilled grills/dangerous exposés/toked pleas/sizzling

90

sonnets/decaffeinations/frustrations/protestations/android
    manuscripts
of maniacal bombast/bomb-blasts of insult poetries/inductions/
    deductions/
colloquial innocence in coopered square journal/rooftop saucers
    catching
the rain of it all/the boredoms/the tapes of el mess/infantile hurls
    of headtrips hurtling thru New York/thru demagnetized zone
    of dead citizenry
the main thing almost forgot/flea market whites sinking in ooze
    of bigotry/
in fear/in meditated memories unfairly marketed in frisks of alarm/
to discard or all lose mind in revelation/in stiff-necked spasm of
    rule-
book definition/into urinary stimulation/into movement/into
    public transportation/
into jazz streets/into rock streets/into sweet memories/into
    transcribing transcendent etymologies of transfusion/into
    tweets of joy/
of bouncing breasts/into theatres of street/gemini positions/
    Genets/ Ornettes/Mingus/Coltrane blue diamonds' glowing
    with Blakelite marched
ideas to beware/what to see/to feel/to do/to behold in wonder/
    to wander
with/run on/in/around/tune into FM/do the Happy Hour/sit
    sweating in
Mexican hot-pepper café/look out thru tortilla window on 2nd Ave.
dipping illusions into spice dish/beer upon beer/illusions become
    reality/
eyelids closing on jointed images/nothing matters in long run/
    what seen/
what remembered/Now & then splits into infinitives/zen-bashed
    hive of fig-
weets/earth-sips of remembrance/rearrangements/things put
    back into
perspective of whine-jug holding images into slowdowns/hits on
    rite-keys
to develop a role/marks of engagement/cannoned copies with
    balls of fire
addictions drumming brush strokes/a smoking/a yardbird
    memorial circulates/
a going on to a further task

Telefone Blues

for Earl Robinson (1910-1991)

Returning your call
            i should say,
"please sing to me, move your voice
into my ear,
         i want to hear your joy,
                 your tears."
'There's no information,
           that's why i call,
to let you know,
        no unamerican inspector comes,
or should,
       however intense the spy-sky becomes,
as painted-by the media.
           Body gone, gone,
it was love for America,
        your immoveable position.
i am going away soon, too,
           i think
             but like
Ginsberg's HOWL
        gone into a third generation
as your song has,
        and further,
          never will be
            enough.
But still having energy for these things,
            i decide to invest
in your BALLAD FOR AMERICA,
         and your JOE HILL.
You know there are connections.
There should be a singing thru telefone.
            i find it
difficult at times,
      the shoutings,
        the buzzing
          and whine,

the news heard all way from Seattle
                         to New Jersey,
and your voice coming thru it all.
                         The sound is deafening.
It is your poetry-soul
                 that brings us,
                         the U.S.A. up to date.
It is deafening.
                 And like poor Joe Hill,
your telefone's been turned off.
                         i got
the telefone blues,
                 but Earl,
                         your voice does
        go on
                 and on
                         and on
                         and on ....

The Horse Is Out On Bail

too many martoonies
located in the rear of the base
its a bitch to ride out
altho you finally realize the pitch is made
out of melted tunes set in a forest of girlscouts
wearing nothing but the right margin of rich
senior testes and gladiolas
poets all
you know the rest is history his story
sorry about that the occasion
is usually spelled wrong
and wong wrung out of words
egyptian carols
shards of garbage
if you know what i am sayin'
the combined district is set in wrung remarks
crayola cabanas hung up on topical trees par avion
steroidal rather than a rithm paramount to furlough
as the DOW prepps in a webster's cough-drop hall
CREMATION i bet you thought
i was going to say CREATION
anything i do say will not be held against me
as i am continuing to ride
on the right margin far from futility
and other electric gasses that go up and down
around dales
poetry hotshots who long for short lines with no meaning
who go on poetry strikes whining to get NEA grants
who wind up with horseshoe around neck
and neighing votes of no confidence
who seek to confide
to lie untracked
who get out on bail
bitter bits of mouth

5/14/98

St. John The Divine Cathedral N.Y.C.
Doings for Allen Ginsberg

110th St. Upper Broadway, N.Y.C.
a huge white mobile media truck
twice the size of westward ho like in
pioneer covered wagons cowboy movies
many men hauling electric cables
utility vehicles in support modern mules
roped-off areas patrolled by walky-talky police
and wooden horses
thousands of young people making scene
come to gape
to celebrate TV Seinfeld network show exit
with wires wires wires wires wires wires
weird world wiring products into American mind
Seinfeld Seinfeld Seinfeld Seinfeld
American national comedy hero chanelled 90's legacy
while two blocks away at St. John The Divine Cathedral
on the front steps a group of Haré Krishna's
chanting Haré Krishna   Haré Krishna   Haré Krishna
Rama Krishna Rama Rama Rama Haré Haré
O WHERE IS KRISHNA THIS NITE

in St. John's Cathedral   Bob Rosenthal   Ed Sanders
Natalie Merchant   MEGA MEGA MEGA   Anne Waldman
and Philip Glass singing a Ginsberg Bop-opera
Patti Smith prostrate on stage with clarinet
screeching   howling   crying   for Allen Ginsberg
sweat and saliva dripping
chanting and rocking and jiving
driving singing crying wanting to dance
and nearly 3,000 souls rise to rock the space
to release personal spiritual energy into the All
into cathedral belly
and hi-charged Andy Clausen bardic singing
and sweet-sung Steven Taylor on Allen's red harmonium

singing Blake while Eliot Katz shares great social concern
and The Fugs The Fugs The Fugs
Ed Sanders   Tuli Kupferberg   Scott Petito & Colby Batty
just Fugging around
and a voice heard at beginning
said Seinfeld was about Nothing
Ginsberg about Everything
O Haré Krishna Krishna Krishna Haré Haré Haré
Rama Rama Rama Rama Rama Krishna Krishna Krishna
in which place were you this nite

5/16/98

High on the Beats

Ode To LAUGH

There'll be laughter in all the plumbed homes.
spontaneous hee ho ha's singing scramble-egg Pollack
    ketchupped platters,
O cackly lite tickling mother's celestial dreams
blinding the maelstrom bolts of rosy tenders,
i quote young eagles, and eastern peckers.
O crackled salve of eczema'd Jersey
you, Laugh, earth's weird tummy tickler swinging thousands
yea, millions of fluorescent souls,
i scream by you, cream by you
i cannot scale my guy-wire wits without inflating your dimension
You collapse in tumbles of crazy teardrops freer than vested
    khans or mended constitutions –
O let there be detective monkeys in every store
and silvery stars in every dream
Buddha in the Capitol contemplating Congress
Gandhi in Dix for basic training
Moses DeMille selling bibles
let there be anty sandy picnic wooded laughter
Kodak Keystone Polaroid pantheistic landscapes
hilarious funhouse roaring-20 women howling pre-babelian toilet
    seats
I laugh lovely as the clacking tubercular fits of subway markers
lovely as my first barbershop
even as my curly locks forever tumble from their strength
yea, even as i kneel in attitude of love
i prophesy a guffaw a day, a blast a week –
O laugh invested with the holy power of an American Deity
you outduel death in your mighty chuckling chamber
O give me this life my fresh bananas
deliver daily shipments of all-bran chortles
manufacture laughing Wall St. stocks
replenish any diminished supply of salesman-giggles
and inscribe me now in the Book of Laughs –

To A Young Poet

If I should insult you,
tell you emphatically
your poetry is split
like your personality
into a hopeless mulch
unable to nourish modernity
this late 20th century,
that it attempts to do the twist
to symphonic operatic status quos
unable to grow soundly
with street tunes
planted in the East Village soil,
attempting to rock n roll
in waltz time
unable to reverse language
to deconstruct
to play creatively with words
or emote animalistic,
even bring oneself
to turn postal stamps
upside-down
to declare love,
or even to declare pain,
but only to run away,
to attempt to modify
natural behavior,
to believe in kissing
both cheeks dutifully
ceremoniously
instead of opening,
pressing lips trustfully,
or splitting mind into bits
analyzing
rather than being joyful,
well then
I could probably
do a number on you

insult your playground makeup,
laugh at your reticence
insolently
and demand
you trash your Beethoven
and trade your university
for the street,
and I could demand
you plug into the Jazz message
massage your consciousness,
well then,
I would be nothing
but a prick
puncturing your reflexive
classical apprehensions,
and I could enjoy your dilemma
momentarily,
then be bewildered with guilt
knowing myself to be cruel
and I know I lack
killer instinct;
so I'd only be hurting myself
insulting you –

from A ROOF OVER CUBA

— for Margaret Randall

1.
a storm is brewed.
a house should have but one roof.
there is no message in the burning myrtle,
                                    it is,
it is so natural to touch it.
in sleep
        the aching fingers
remember the heat that this pain
                        cries for,
that those who stay at home
                    will show up green
that this storm is different
                in its way,
it grins in its eye
                arrives
                unnervingly.
the moon smiles at such times,
at free men.
here, in the hurt flesh
                there is communication.

4.
my gun is rusty,
disused,
once it created revolution,
the beginning of a new world,
and a language of love,
but, i must say,
        "you are old now,
i don't need you old friend,
there is no place to go with you."
i use words now
and listen to the chattering letters
cast up out of this steel-mouth typewriter.

5.
there in moncada
a fifteen year old girl
                had a party,
a girl who would wipe the sun's blood
                             from her eyes
                                 at twenty-one.
a crazy suffering stretched her mouth in song,
in victory
        the fat hand
               would reap her years
scorched within a uniform
                   covered with blood.
there was a carnival of death at moncada
in a house meant for farmers.

i am poet

in the real city of poetry
all the homes are spoken poems
landscaped with ultra brite jazzy flowers

i am poet
priest of greenfused atomic youth
damned and doomed to speak technologies
my vision a babbling liquid oxygen tower
a tryst of man to screw the sky

i am poet
caesar of a legion's lost emotions
tied and trowelled to try people's patience
my meal an earthly smorgasbord
a one-world-platter of human meat
a sour rumbling atomic indigestion

O i am poet launching childrens' doom
from my voiceless scribbler's pad
my sound a falling autumn leaf
raked by the sky-king critics
to burn in quaking city fate

O i am poet
digging liteless sonic booms
& fall-out words that split in air
my dead-end fist in soft retreat
shoed by orbital visions
as my trembling fingers clutch at life

3/13/74

5:35 am
in Bayonne
riding my English-make
Royal Scot bicycle
crosstown on 33rd St.
chanting my morning prayer
to evoke God Spirit
to make positive intention
that i live this day
but once
& with right attitude
hope & luck & God
a good day,
chanting haré Krishna
haré Krishna
haré Rama haré Rama
Krishna Krishna
haré haré haré haré
Krishna,
going west
peddling uphill
cars parked diagonally
tree-lined street quiet
sparrows chirping
going past Baumuller Funeral Home
old landmark
used to tell Ted Enslin
how close he was to my Bayonne home,
loss of brilliance
bicycle needing new batteries for light,
windy this morning
makes peddling difficult uphill;
small brown coyote dog stands still
in middle of street
pointing to singing birds
who welcome God with song-voice
singing for food and water,

O Krishna be kind to the birds today,
lead them to my backyard
where'll be breadcrumbs in bushes,
approaching Kennedy Boulevard
peak of trip,
think of St. Marks Church reading this nite,
McClure and Ginsberg
McClure myth out of *Evergreen Review,*
Book of Torture & Ghost Tantras,
Ginsberg simpatico old penpal
multi god-prophet
headline synthesizer
see him synthesizing Tom Paine,
Jefferson, Thoreau,
Franklin inventor of electric words,
also zenny laughing god of poetry
hi-charged bell ringer
discovering America
482 years after Columbus
this moment in Bayonne 5:38 am
on westside Bayonne, Avenue A
nearing my hip blue candystore
birds singing
celebrating Day
wind blows same reason,
tonite if all is well
i go to St. Marks,
if too tired and don't go
I chant alone on bicycle
eastward
and say la vie
la vie
sad la vie
but hope springs eternal
pulse runs sure
i rise from business
earning money
take time to pray
and laugh
and maybe streak in church

in head
an inside-out hasid chanting Krishna,
a sparrow pecks red licorice-stick
on sidewalk amid gum-lumps
in front of store,
i squeeze handbrakes
come to halt
and reach for keys to store,
O Krishna Krishna
God-friend
bring a good day

ANTARCTICA

Map #1

Tico tico pop art calls for way to map
National Cape F.G. Beelinghausen qualude
                                    circumnavigation
        oy vay
            may be Russian.

Seal Bay division chief Garver old Beat
        buddy on iceshelf Norged in Mexico 1960.

All this produced by Wilbur 2 r's 2 t's Garrett
hung up on the Cartographic Shit division
sealed bay 10 degrees longitude
Atka Kraul Iceport
no doubt about
Kilroy was there with German George von Meyer
between war and movie starring Bernadette Mayer
in which she wears a boa O boy
Passat Boreas Cum squat
the plot abt squats who freeze off their
                                    hemorrhoids

and Gilbert Gross Venor circum sized
                            in his upper class
even if President & Chairman of the Great
                                    Society
along with Garrett 2r's 2t's Ever Sharpe
O poop poop a doop just numbers
421 524 1451 4000 220 1820 go
pick-3 pick-4 win a continent
            but
don't be west of Greenwich or Borg
or climb Mt Haligren
            or
be caught in the light and be tanned
be sent out hungry with pan
it is gold they're all
after all —

Map #2

New York to Archipelago
        thru eyes of Mr. Coffee
chief arbiter of the Southwest whatever
it's hot that's what
Nevada Valley stretches Sierra Truth

I hear thunderous drums
        play Mr. Bangs
        Mount 2442 purplish notes
blow ole nose
squeeze right side

A & P Iron nipple Mission
serves Mormon salad whatever
it was biblical indicated
                        dictated by u know
WHO
like Virgin mountains
humpted over Dixie
with big banged ears boxed with God
high on Norman Peak 2259 feet
I assume stance riding old Pinto
thru Beatitude altitude

all poems now done with Workshop Approach
an Enterprise not a ship
        either
but with pleasant surprise –

Code Blue
(Bokar Tov)

Ears listening to Israeli sounds
swish swoosh traffic sounds
sweat runs down face and down neck
and from under arms and down back and belly

sonic booms sonic booms sonic booms
bokar tov
jet doves break sound barrier over Jordan water
dread lilts of military
thoughts go blue
come on the blue bus
blue terminal
blue sea
blue ships in the blue harbor
blue heat
blue-stressed people
blue bazaar language of wizards
blue Israeli love letters
aleph bases
blue notes hung bending deja vu
blue racial memory stuffed in blue tallis bag
blue mind maps tourist information
blue military wares
and passport to the promised land
blue cancellations in this meshugennah world
blue spy inquiry
blue Iraqian energy-snake rattling Kuwait
blue what's happening
blue briefing
blue mortars blue tanks a lot
blue army sacrifice on war alter
blue widows and orphans
blue store of water in blue bomb shelter
blue killer missiles to scud with blue gas
for blue babies, zaydies and bubbies

blue bolts of lightning
blue balls of fire
blue-boggled world boiling with lack of information
blue indignation
and blue imagined monsters
blue bonds binding family wounds
posthumous blue boxes of ribbons and medals
blue bricolage catapulting blue death balls
blue regulations
blue thoughts come in mind full of fear
blue Iraqian anxieties
I want to cut up what's-his-name
Saddam!
sad damn situation come down to
oil-drunk greedy egos clank and crank toward war
as mid-east radio speaks hearsay
thru gas-mask images
as the innocent & the not-so-innocent
ride the black-gold express
on way to heaven or hell
O bokar tov   bokar tov   bokar tov   alright
will Baghdad turn to ash
will Haifa go breathless
and Israel become only a Mediterranean meditation
OH   MY   GOD!!!!!

The Sad Jack Kerouac Buddha Blues

I got the Sad Jack Kerouac Buddha Blues
got the Sad Jack Kerouac Buddha Blues

I've got the October bare tree blues
the November bare tree blues

O how it seems like only yesterday
or maybe it was really tomorrow
Jack Kerouac packed, picked up his rucksack
filled it full of Love and Celebration
went on his storied road, satoried, storied
and sang his songs of Self and Pelf
sang his songs of Self and Pelf

Every time a railroad whistles here in Zenville
I buy a ticket to the Buddha Blues

Every time a politician speaks
I get alarmed and stroke the cat

O how sad I am this November
I got the bare tree blues
I got the bare tree blues

The Lonesome Traveller gone these many years
The Lonesome Traveller gone these many years

I got the Sad Jack Kerouac Buddha Blues
I got the Sad Jack Kerouac Buddha Blues

This Song Is For You

It's April in Paris
and I'm flyin' the friendly sky,
can't seem to make up my mind,
O my melancholy baby
I'm undecided now,
for you took away my heart
and now I've got the hesitation blues,
can't seem to make up my mind,
you could be my jazz baby
beyond the blue horizon,
you could be my satin doll
until I wouldn't know what time it is

O baby, you stir my fire
and I'm just sayin' gimme time
gimme time, baby-face,
'cause I've got the hesitation blues
and my song is for you
everywhere that flamingos fly.
You could be my Janis, my Billie,
and I could be your Bobby McGee,
but I'm still tryin' to tame the lion for real
doin' the oney musk farewell to whiskey
and stompin' at the Savoy,
so even tho the heat is on,
and I'm buried alive in the blues
and afraid of a second time around,
I just can't make up my mind
even knowing there'll never be another you,
it's as simple as that,
just one of those things
like blues in the nite

I think I'll have to get out of town,
go about 500 miles away
all boogied out and bewildered,
so for now, I'm just sayin'
I'm undecided now, but remember,
love can move mountains
and this song is for you

Go Man, Go

— for Alan Kaufman

Yeah, go man, go
go to yer great fate
appointment,
go, drive, please,
I mean spin out,
eat the future now,
I mean peel out yer soul,
I mean go with god-spirit,
yer Self,
make yer connections,
drive, drive, drive man,
buzz off yer solitude –

Go man, go,
rev up yer priorities,
yer Poetry,
yer empathetic soul,
yer hot, heavy, heaving
breath of hetero
Harley-sparked emotion –

Go man, go,
burn in yer sterno-mind,
in the great American nite –

Yeah, go man, go,
barrel out
across American consciousness,
cruise with yer muse,
use eye and ear,
record America,
tap, trap sound,
and sing Whitmanic song
of the states,
the rocking rolling
roiling, railing,

hungry melting pot,
the nite bars,
the wail bars,
the sad diners
coast to coast,
the sweet lullabies
that turn to toast –

Yeah, go man, go,
cross the Missississipi,
go West, go man,
cross the heartland,
and swear to live crazy
raging like a wetback
turned back at the border
by bitter blue customs –

Go man, go howl
yer commentary,
yer frustration
and American Pities –

Yeah, go, drive,
ride on the tale of a poem,
ride the wail express,
ride with John Coltrane,
do the Greyhound cha cha
yer adrenalin flowing
with depression,
its nitemare chat-a-nooging
across America's
sensitive skull –

Be flexible
as lies circulate
in this promised land,
hid in the scum of Hope,
as a national Dope-Control
Machine sets up
surrepticiously

to fix the needy concepts
to build prisons
and deny the vote
across America
demonizing
as souls are burgled
and pulled down, covered,
with the shades of TV news –

Yeah, go man, go,
ride 'em poem-boy,
be eephus, silas
a silent ichabod,
be a 200 year apparition
riding on the Bill of Rites
yer curled chords blasting
cacaphonical
thru hunger's stereo-type –

Yeah, go man, go,
saddle up yer dream-wheels,
go, cross Whitman's horizon,
go hurtling,
spurting dreams,
go wild,
screech Cyborgian
yippity-do-dahs,
go spin yer psychedelicate dreams,
go American poet-statesman,
legislate this awful slump
out of existence,
bump it off dramatic
like man on the moon –

Yeah, go paranoid, man,
go understand,
be acute, aware of
ultimate death-obsessions,
and the bop
of freedom's suicide,

Hope's heartbeat tapering off,
exhausted,
its old ghost
of exhilaration
been caricatured,
comical Caspered,
castrated in
Chagallian ecstatic
perceptions
like broken glass bits –

Yeah, go man,
go into Essence of Soul,
go rescue this race,
meditate it healthy,
speak it so –

Yeah, go man,
go American on High Way,
Yeah, make yer
Heavenly Connection,
to the corner of Be-Kind
and Be-Compassionate –

Yeah, go man,
go dream America,
go on, go on, go on,
go on before you wake –

Hither & Dither & Yon
On A Lucid Moon

I croon this toon
for the men on the lucid moon
Neil & Ralph
and Al Phalpha
a rap for the hot hip hoppers
boppers
beating their gums
with silvery spoons
calling for poems
from Santa Claus
because exactly to say
this trip suddenly takes
on a different perspective
Poetry is the Desire
the Disease
and misses the mark
whatever that is
and collects a downtown diary
of barbaric yelps
yawps
rants-in-the-pants
I am afraid
of the year 2000
afraid to recall
all the empty promises
made in a wave of euphoria
when I was chasing rainbows
so it goes
looking back with Lot's wife
while the dish on the roof
aimed at the moon
raised new hopes
long live insecurity
long live blabbery net-verbs
long live blubbery net-webs

long live rubbery blurbs
and coming up tonite
there'll be telefone crooks
selling the Great Passaic Falls
lucid midnite frills
frick frack funky foos
chips of the titles come thru space
falling falling falling
falling in electric attitudes
blue ludes
circled by poetic ravens
the story is a dirty pow-wow
all hearts to dance lustily
to this lucid toon
smoking from ham town
to rte 66
to Joplin misery
punkie dorrie
where poets pull down pants
to get on a moon
where lonely love is no delusion
is just a little old ditty
a promise to dance thru life
is it all for nothing
to sing moonie isolation blues
loose and lucid
go out of earthly bounds
mooning and moaning
crooning
and flying high
hither and dither and yon

pinched verbs

— for Steve Hartman

to pinch verbs that pinch nerves/to wish to believe/to spew frick-fracked saturday emptiness/to demolish the possibility of wanting to spend energy/to keel over and to bury time/to party chained to circumstance/or dance with curtained dreams/to think to prove oneself thru poetry/to erase all this/to piss on it all/and to believe and to disbelieve in a chain of pinched-nerve events taken from woolworth counters/to feel like a prince of pinched-verb possibilities forgetting the fire last time/forever seduced by a sagitarius missing an o/and to party ending up in pain/and to live life under a strain/to spend energy stretching silent screams from a pinched faucet of tears/stolen from dreams/and to erase it all/to spit on it all/to dance saturday nites trashing pinched nerves looking for a quick nynex telefone fix/a heavy breath seduction/a smoking date firing salvos of pinched verbs while walking thru new york's crime square circus/and to go day-glo painting/to collage the new york skyline with a swaggery tongue/to lullaby and bury brooklyn nicotined on welfare/to erase all this and go on to party as if there's no tomorrow/and to spit out pinched verbs/to spew nervous verbs/to kneel verbing on an f-train to brooklyn pledging never to ride one again thru the neurotic brooklyn nite/and to cry switchblades guns crack-heads/and to erase all this/and to pour out soul/to cough disembodied beneath brooklyn's red neon rainbow/and to be anonymous/to pass out pinched verbs on subway platforms/to grind up aggravations into latex yoga positions/to sing/to steal verbs/to read allen ginsberg and get high agreeing with him/and to erase all this and to blame no one but blame everyone/as the sun rises over bay ridge/and to count your blessings/to count yourself lucky to be a brooklyn cowboy/ to lasso verbs and dance on the page with them/to pinch yourself and know you are alive/and never to erase the great poet-spirit that drives you thru the brooklyn nite/

THE DEVIL'S IN THE PALM OF MY HAND

I CROSS OUT LETTERS IN THE WORDS
ON THE PALM OF MY HAND
TO CHANGE STRUCTURE
BUT CANNOT SEEM TO MAKE IT WORK
SO I HOST A POEM
OR GO TO ANN GREY'S
TO HOIST ONE OR TWO
AND CREATE A POEM WITH RANDOM CHOICES
DO YOU KNOW WHAT I'M SAYIN?
I'VE BECOME A FLUID PHYSICAL LANGUAGE ASSASSIN
I STICK MY STYLUS INTO THE LANGUAGE INDUSTRY
I WOUND T.S.ELIOT IN HIS WASTELAND
AND POETRY STARS COME OUT TO SING IN ALABAMA
THEN SUDDENLY THE DEVIL APPEARS
BACK FROM HIS VACATION IN THE DEEP BLUE SEA
BUT STILL SPOUTING HYSTERICAL INDIAN CONSPIRACIES
AND SWEARING HE'S QUIT TOBACCO
FOR THE OTHER STUFF
AND UPON INVITATION BY THE ALDINGTONS
THAT'S MR AND MRS RICHARD I PRESUME
HE (DEVIL) GROWS HIS HAIR LONG
AND WEARS AN APRON
CHANGES HIS NAME TO ST. SULPICE
JOINS THE STYLISH INFANTRY AS AN IKE OF THE FUTURE
MEANWHILE PREPARING A FATAL BARBECUE DINNER
FOR SHIPFITTER PRIVATES
MAKING OBSCENE OMELETTES WITH HYSTERICAL
ABANDONED OVARIES
THE OTHER MAIN INGREDIENT ASIDE FROM THE MISLAID EGGS
ARE LARRY EIGNER'S STUTTERING WORDS
THAT I HOLD IN MY PALM
TO STICK UP THE DEVIL'S NOSE
THAT ET CETERA BASTARD
WHO PRETENDED TO BE THE VIRGILION JAKOMAN ROBSON
OR ANOTHER NEAL CASSADY KING OF PARKING LOTS
SO LONG DEVIL IN MY PALM
I DRUM YOU OUT OF THE INFANTRY
YOU ARE A SHAME TO THE BRIGHTNESS OF HAIR
A WASTE   A SHAME   A SHAM   A WORD   A NAME

THE AMTRAK BLUES

BABY OH OH OOH BABY BABY BABY BABY
GOIN TO ATLANTA GOIN TO ATLANTA
GEORGIA ON MY MIND GEORGIA ON MY MIND
JIMMY GIUFFRE SHOUT'N HEAD GIUFFRE SHOUT'N HEAD
GOIN WAY GOIN WAY GOIN WAY
LEROY VINEGAR PLUCK'N VINEGAR PLUCK'N
GERRY MULLIGAN SING'N MULLIGAN SING'N
A SAX N CRESCENT SOUND SAX N CRESCENT SOUND
GOIN TO ATLANTA ON THIS CRESCENT TRAIN

BABY OH BABY OH BABY BABY OOH
GOT THE AMTRAK BLUES GOT THE AMTRAK BLUES
THE NITE VISION BLUES NITE VISION BLUES
SLIM WHITE SLACKS ROUND ROUND BREASTS
OH OOH OOH GOT THE GOLD EARING BLUES
THE HUNGRY CURL'N BENT-BODY BLUES
HUNGRY CURL'N BENT BODY BLUES
THE NEWARK NEW JERSEY ATLANTA BLUES

BABY BABY OH OOH BABY
NOW NOW NOW NOW NOW GOT THE AMTRAK BLUES
THE AMTRAK BLUES AMTRAK BLUES
A-SHARIN THE SEAT SHARIN SHARIN THE SEAT
WITH A NITE-VISION VAMP NITE VISION VAMP
SET ME ON FIRE ON FIRE ON FIRE
GOT THE AMTRAK BLUES AMTRAK BLUES
THE BLUES IN THE NITE BLUES IN THE NITE

O BABY OH BABY GOT THE AMTRAK BLUES
DONT MIND THE LURCH'N THE LURCH'N
DONT MIND THE OVERHEAD LITE
OVERHEAD LITE SHININ ON MY DREAM
DONT MIND THE STIFF ACHIN LEGS
STIFF ACHIN LEGS
LONG AS YOU SO SWEET LONG AS YOU SO SWEET
LONG AS YOU SO WARM   SO WARM
NEXT TO ME   NEXT TO ME
ON THE AMTRAK SEAT   ON THE AMTRAK SEAT

NOW NOW NOW NOW BABY BABY NOW BABY
GOT THE AMTRAK BLUES   THE AMTRAK BLUES
THE HANDS OFF BLUES   HANDS OFF BLUES
MY HEAD FULL OF DESIRE   HEAD FULL OF DESIRE
ON THE LITTLE WHITE PILLOW   THE LITTLE WHITE PILLOW
GOT THE HANDS OFF BLUES   HANDS OFF BLUES
THE AMTRAK BLUES   THE AMTRAK BLUES
A M T R A K   B L U E S

Oh Well Determination On A Gray Day

— for Joyce Metzger

This day Quando la Luna
merges in my heart
with a froggy hoarse voice
singing a sad Jack Kerouac Buddha Blues
in a JVC ZZZZYNE

I take a really good look
at my gloomy website
as the weather outside grows stormy
and determine to write to the bone
and suck the sweet marrow of morn
for the sun to shine on my art

Life is sweet
and art can be a song
and even this croaky frog-voice
be exorcised with shadowy shades
and there'll be sweet tidings no bull

My song will mock this acid world
and I'll press smiles into my calculator
feed my poems with Quando la Luna
and put shine back on my brain-block

At least at present its possible
but how did a frog get into this

Oh well

Dream Galaxie

— for Perry Robinson

to love   to say   to speak   to fold   & unfold clouds
to reach into sound
           to stretch
                to be pied-pipered
dude-of-universe
           eternal note-master
                  musical
hot-trotter
      to be spot translator of Way
                to paint
earth-colored sounds
          to be van Gogh
              Braque
Jackson Pollack
      to do Own Thing
           sing bio Buddha-notes
voice-clefs
      to rivet infrastructure
           to whirl pearl
to knit future
      all hail clarinet   as power
as applause
      as raw roar
        to see
          saw
            to hear
recognize beeps
        bleats
        blurts
           to bend all over
to see jets below clouds
          to bend zen-shaped moans
into wondrous tones
        to shape lightning emptors
illuminated glows
      to hear Freiberg lyricals

hot tradie jazz magics
                    in deck of serious jokers
spinning   spinning   spinning   spinning spies
in sky
        sunset spooks
                    in dream-notes
                                    mailed
from eternal heavenly space
                            in cascades
                                        sprays
of hilarious joys
                and hail-storm sound-sheets
oh   oh   the bandstand shrieks
                            oh the taut
panasonical throat-tokes
                    oh to toss zen beatifics
to dial smiles
            to play the future
                            take a walk on the moon
go musically thru milky way
                        thru yelpy blues black
beat crashings
            thru bruised perceptions
thru ethereal sensations
                        thru thunder and Hampelling
trampelling
        stomping
                boom boom
                        reverberations
vibraphonic earth-turnings
                        lightning meat-notes
lists of lusts
            New-age post modern celestial launchings
lunch on Venus
                dinner on Mars
                            musical bars
sound embraces in emotional halls of longing
                        long pronged long gone shudders

& hot mentholy chills
    up
       down
          spine
    a bald eagle shrieking in sound attack
a singing
       song
          a white-caged tenor
                  a madness
an ultimate flite to a breached horizon
                  a bleeding
in knitting factory
            in an unknowable screwed universe
into
    out of
       a musician's magic mind
               to play festive
Perry Gabriel Angel
          lists visions
             emotions
              horn
explosions
    his hip ear
       mind
          structures sound
& rhythm
    changing chords
          twisting
          swirling
           whirling
curling
    bending body into future musical trips
back and forth
       across continents
          back into memory-womb
toes on earth
    eyes in heaven
       knitting brows
          lips

flowing thru space
                    vibrant
                            ringing celestial numbers
drum beating
            jazz magic
                    bopping
                            clopping
                                    oh   oh
jazz-gaze into craze of future
                    be powerful
time-warps
        knitting sounds in black satin nite
pulsing
    yelping
            howling thru electronic speaker
into red eye of video
                    to whisper
                            to offer
stored images
            thru licorice disc
                            to be powered
by applause
        to whirl into future
                            to sing bio-notes
rivet life's infrastructure
                    like Van Gogh
                            Braque
Jackson Pollack
        paint way to heaven
                            space out
eternity
    reach for sound
                unfold clouds in mind
to be able to say with music
                    all is but a dream —

Cittee Cittee Cittee IV

— *In Memory of Abe Lebewohl*

In New York ah go see Manhattan spectacle cittee
go see gee East village holee molee cittee cittee
see Big Apple American avant empire gridlock gentrify cittee
pyramid cittee millennium cittee renewable cittee
see cittee of worshipping churches synagogues and mosques
yes yes re in carnation cittee
entertainment cittee museum cittee medallion taxi cittee
waterway cittee Hudson Harlem East River bay and inlet cittee
ferryboat cittee foodcart cittee fashion cittee
bargain niknak paddywak thums-up cittee & tums down cittee
Mets Yankee Knick Islander playground cittee cittee
Greyhound Trailways cittee bridge and tunnel cittee
park and zoo cittee subway cittee ferry terminal cittee
Wall St cittee big bank Federal Reserve cittee
YMHA YMCA YWCA YWHA health club cittee
free concert cittee opera cittee sidewalk musician cittee
artist cittee poet-writer rock and jazzee cittee
ah go East Village see taxees racing braking screeching
honking hear emergencee ambulance sireen screeming
get outta way a sudden heartattack cittee a natural cittee
a be-where kamakazee ghost-rider bicycle whooshing cittee
cut thru the nite sometimes with whistle warning
cittee where sidewalks hardly ever empty
cittee of constant movement cittee where Lower Manhattan
synagogues stand forlorn empty congregants moved uptown
or to suburban nirvanas or Florida deceased
and in East village sidewalk corner 2nd Ave 10th St
Yiddish stars of past names embedded in sidewalk
ah sweet memorees O Molly Picon New York echoes Hollywood
O New York Empire Kosher Kasatska Simcha Cittee Cittee
O 2nd Ave Deli with Molly Picon dining roan O cittee
O cittee of ex-mayor would-be governor now columnist & judge
Ed Koch a nice New Ark New Jersey Yiddisha boy-chick
O cittee of Allen Ginsberg also born New Ark cittee
become Daddy of cittee cittee poets seeking dharma

Allen a Jewish Cultural American Buddhist ikon in cittee
O Hebrew National Empire Kosher cittee answering to a
higher authority in everchanging cittee cittee
O fearful joyful farful farflung underground
subway economy cittee
O 2nd Ave Gutterman funeral home where Phillip Glass
played Mickey Ruskin Memorial and der newspaper FORWARTZ
Bintel Brief memoree I.B.Singer lookin back this was
the Life in Lower East Side New York Cittee
and now drygood pushcart sidewalk vendors talk Spanish
Orchard St Nuyoricans selling buying sneakers underwear
and schlock shops sell bohemians bloopered clothing
nothing too fancy on Delancey St New York cittee
and now 6th St Community sin-a-gog overflows Lubavitcher
Cooper Union youth congregation with Shabbos dinner
and old widowers chant kaddish celebrate G-d in E.Village
O Beat Generation Runaway cittee of Love & vcr's
and Bob Dylan acoustic on way to American Starland
O Schimel cittee of potato onion kasha knisheree
kabosheree tahkee tahkee as Houston St gridlock continues
O bagel bialee roogalach cittee Bialistocker kuchen cittee
home of Moishe's homemade motesee braided challah
and fancy bowtie cittee where Yom Kippur annual New York
cittee becomes Lamentation cittee
where children of all ages munch pizza falafel tandooree
O Brother kilbassa peerogeez blintzes burgers chickee chickee
buffalo wingees hot dogs with the works
mustard and kraut strings hanging out to eternitee
O my bistu shayna cittee cittee
O Autumn-colored cittee of smoked salmon platter
and neighborhood chatter O cittee of hip yuppees
and yuppee hippees O sireenee screechee clangee sleezee cittee
wheezee cittee squeegee windshield cittee cittee
onion chop cholesterolee cittee and gefilta-fish
horseradish East Village tears of Joyous Kings & Queens
celebrating latkeh legends while salivating heroicalleee
who with each enjoyable geshmeck lick applesauce lips
while on East Houston St the Homeless roast ashcan mickees
O Mah-neesh-tahna cittee ainkelohaino cittee
where Streit's matzoh bakeree beckons New York cittee

and Schapiro's wineree holding bottled boray pree hagoffen
and on 2nd Ave Israelee Rectangle restaurant sidewalk cous
cous while famous 2nd Ave Deli delites in stuffed cabbage
onion mushroom garlic salami & eggs in delicious high
so what cittee O Yiddish-kite meta fold frolic in
amazing sometimes haiku cittee O Allen Ginsberg
Buddhist Cultural Jew eulogized in Christian Poetry
Project Church while outside church is Abe Lebewohl Park
Abe's presence awaiting Justice O ruach cittee
Orchidia Bar gentrified cittee unfinished subway dream
cittee 2nd Ave O thick lentil soup with carrots afloat
in vitamin A cittee all amidst an ailee ailee Menashe
Skolnik memoree cittee and cittee now resonates yoohoo
to Loisaida babaloo to you cittee and kabob kabob
kabob kabop kabop in co-op cittee cittee where medium
rare with mash potato is often the fare in cittee
O chop liver 2nd Ave Deli free hors doevres for appetizer
in skyrocket rental cittee where Veselka newsstand had
bad news Tienamen Square while sidewalk crowds walk
cittee in peace St. Marks Place where Zen sushi sold
and pita and pizza and Afghan soulfood where underground
tapes & cd's comic books & outrageous cittee t-shirts
shades & jewelry & Gem Spa cigar/candystore video game
bing bing bing cittee cittee where chocolate eggcream
dreams are fulfilled across from moneymachine bank
near Ukranian Home Restaurant serving the best chopped
beet salad & the old hotel called by a poet The Cittee
Terradome where outside a group of heavymetal people with
Mohawk-heads hang out with their ears nose lips tongues
and what else hanging pierced with gold earrings and
up the block around the corner on 3rd Ave the St Marks
Bookstore with Allen Ginsberg's books in window and
the old Grassroots Tavern down the block that Allen
pointed out years ago and on 2nd Ave the famous B & H Dairy
restaurant with special soup of day served with biggest
hunk of buttered challah-toast and in middle of block
St Marks Pl the old Ukranian Hall become The Electric Circus
now a rehab center hangout for drop-outs doing
arts and crafts and something missing on 2nd Ave whatever
happened to Fillmore East O this ever-changing cittee

where stores come and go like yellow cabs O street
festival cittee speed cittee whistling bicycle cittee
Village Voice cittee and defunct East Village Other cittee

Tompkins Square Park band-shell memorees and the Homeless
Tent Cittee at times all seem become a video meat cittee
and early 60's pome-vibe-Metro-Cafe now only an echo
in trendee Telefone Bar O Bubbee-blessed Shabbos Chicken
chunkee cholent here Tahttala cittee feeling ill go
slurp 2nd Ave Deli Lebewohl's chickee soup better than
penicillin and with lite as heavenly clouds knaedloch
floating in cittee cittee go down easy East Village be Boho
be Straight be Bi be Gay in everything goes cittee go
condo go co-op go cable be magical in mystical cittee
go see ancient graveyard with traffic whooshing spasmodic
honking cittee go First and Second and Third Aves.
and Alfabet cittee A B C D you bet cittee and get
your numbers zipcode cittee 10003 10009 and telefone
numbers 674 675 477 254 533 475 529 282 all
East Village numbers in New York CITTEE CITTEE CITTEE

This Is The Real Thing

(A Sculpted Painting)
— for Joe Borzotta

White layers of rubber
    set on surface
        sit on world

O baby that's so kool
this is the real thing

The soul's like a fanbelt
        art's on a roll
      frame this visual

O heavenly flower power
a four-houred layer of galactic fame
        hear ye   hear ye
inscribe it with a liquid name
        hang a heavenly dream
           on an off-white pillow
this is the real thing

        hear ye   hear ye
all call for a liquid lift-off
    it is all so kool
    so berry berry kool
    this is the 10 St dimension
a bouquet of flower power
this is the real thing

O come all ye artistes
    stir our souls to satori
      as we go bumping
humping in Hoboken heaven
    our fan belts rolling
      finiculee finicula la la la
        at times screeching

for the key to heaven's gate
this is the real thing

Art fans our soul
bowls us over in a gallery
O sure its a rubbery surreal world
evil fire stones separate lives
the Truth should be All
come look in Aladdin's envelope
All is black and white
this is the real thing

For Yuko Otomo

Bring me your haiku
Let's make love in 17 syllables

Let's drink kava kava
at the head of a cosmic factory table

It's a time to remember

Let's make new the klezmisha babble
the instant comedy of life
and the sharp philosophic piney symbols

Let's reserve a calendar full of
incomplete decisions, directions, and
let's cheer abbakabibble dribbles

Let's sing some blue notes for public illumination

Let's hang out in The Pink Pony Café

Let's get high on the llamas of drudge
the Dodge city shakers

Let's hang late at nite with klezmokum
smoking, stoking, poking fun
in the main spaced

Let's have klezmer at Woodstock
their mod stockings hung on a Buddha limb

Let's have candles stuck on a Hannukah bush
with a shammos on clarinet & a Greene piano

And get it all down
in 17 syllables, more, or less

MICHELINE

O Compassionate Seeker
Weeper
Dream-Bleeder in Futility Bedroom
Love-Needer Neither Here Nor There
Neither Flat Out In A Cold-Water Palace
Or Hot Times in Boulder, Colorado
Who Bird-Love On Road To Imploding America
Who Cried With Joy And Tears
In Each Star-Lit Nite
While Walking With Wind's Caress

O Rainbow Dreamer
Who Dreamt of Enchanted Music
"In Smoke-filled Dens of Arabia"
Who Was King Of The Road To Love
A Child of Spring
"Looking At The Sky"
Crying Tears Of Joy

You Were Only A Bronx Rooster
An Imaginary Yankee
Dynamo Of Street Speech
A Fire-Plugged Poet
Poet Made Of Cloth
A Tortured Pigeon Crying Love Lost In East Village
Weeping As Money Carried The Day
O Pan Aramaic Poet Who Played Bongo
In Bleak American Nite

O Sky-Whammied Muse Diabetic
Who Hung Out San Francisco Nites
A Bronx Rooster Who Clucked Love
Wandering Downtown New York City
To Sing 1/2 Note Songs In A Hudson Street Bar

O Bard Who Let Down Your Guard
Street Singer
Word Flinger Who Gave Money The Finger
Who Dreamt Of Flowing Rivers
And Better Days
Who Used Voice As Weapon of Love
Voice As Soul-Expression
Voice As World-Balm
A Voice Prophetic
Voice Worth A Million A Trillion
Voice Not Soon Forgotten
Voice Flowing From Bronx To San Francisco
Voice Of An Outlaw Forever "Jack-The-Kid"
Voice Laughing Crying Always Trying
Voice Of Grandfather Winter
Voice Of Crucified Tongue
Voice Of Childhood Memories
Voice Of Rivers Flowing
Children Singing Beauty Breathing
Voice Of Jack-Be-Nimble Jack-Be-Quick
Of Jack Who Jumped Over The American Candle Shtick
Voice Of Whitman in Celebration
Voice Of America

3/6 – 3/9/98

SAINTLY

Preface: David Church says,
"Hung out with Bremser
at Cherry Valley Arts Festival,
found him Saintly."

SAY, RAY, YOU AINT NO SAINT ANDREW
    AINT NO ANTHONY
YOU AINT NO AUGUSTINE AINT NO BARNABY
    AINT NO BRUNO
AND GOD FORBID YOU CAINT BE MISTAKEN
      FOR NO CATHERINE
    OR CUTHBERT

HEY, YOU CAN SEE THIS IS GOING ALPHABETICAL
RAY, YOU AINT NO ELMO OR GEORGE OR IGNATIUS
MAYBE AN IGNU POET SAINT
BUT NO SAINT JAMES OR JOHN OR JOSEPH
      AND YOU AINT A MARK
ALTHO YOU ALWAYS BEEN A MAGIC POETRY MARKER
      BUT NO PETER OR PAUL
WE'RE GETTING CLOSE RAY
CAUSE SAINTS ARE BORN AGAIN
AND YOU WENT THRU THAT LOTSA TIMES
HEY, "A FIELD OF WHEAT, A COW, A GOAT,
      RABBIT, SQUIRREL, DOG, & CHICKEN,
      A CHOCOLATE COVERED ANT, FISH,
      BEANS, & DAYLILLIES"
      (DAYLILLIES, RAY?)
RAY, I BET YOU WERE IN BUDDHA'S DREAM
"A CREEPY CATERPILLAR BECOME A BEAUTYFUL
POETRY BUTTERFLY"
AND RAY, YOU FOREVER ON A COMEBACK
WHAM WHAM BAMMING CYMBAL (SYMBOL)
    A BEAT LORD'S BEAT MESSENGER
CAUSE GOD SAY WHAM YOU WHAMMED
    WHAMMED WHAMMED WHAMMED WHAMMED

BAMMED BAMMED AWAY AT YOUR DEMONS
MADE THE PHD'S GET UP AND SCRAM
THEIR DEGREES AND DIPLOMAS IN DISARRAY
WHILE YOUR POETRY CARRIED THE DAY
WALKING WHAMMING TALKING WHAMMING DANCING
      DRINKING WHAMMING
WHAMS FOR BREAKFAST WHAMS FOR LUNCH DINNER
RAY, YOU COMING BACK BE BORN AGAIN
BE BORN ON ROAD TO VILLACAPAMPA
BE JERSEY NOMAD THUMBING THRU AMERICA
    CUTTING THRU GRAMMARIAN JUNGLES TO FREEDOM
      AND IN YUGEN *POEMS OF CITY MADNESS*
WHERE YOU BE BORN TO BE POET
    VICTIM OF PENAL MADNESS
ON ROAD WITH POET CONQUERORS
RAY, RAY, OLD MEMORIES COFFEEHOUSE BEAT POETRY
YOU AND PAUL MUNI, RAY, GASLITE STARS
IN BRIGHTENING JAZZY LOONEY VERSE
WHERE YOUR BONNIE ANGEL STARRED IN YOUR MOVIE
WHILE YOU SAT ON 7 ARTS STAIRWAY TO HEAVEN
DRINKING WINE INTIMATE TALKING SAINTLY YES
AND EARLY MORN RIDING HUDSON BLVD TRANSIT BUS
    TO JERSEY CITY BREMSERLAND
NODDING THRU LINCOLN TUNNEL DREAMING ANGEL
    WRITING JAZZY DREAM POEM
RAY RAY YOU BE A GONE SAINT
YOU "KISHA KISHA KISHA KISHA"
A KOSHER KISHA KOOL POETRY DUDE
"CYMBAL CYMBAL CYMBAL CYMBAL"
YOU SPOKE AND CRACKLED AND SMOKED BOP-CABALA
CONNED AND HUSTLED YOUR WAY THRU
        SUBTERRANEAN AMERICA
YOU WERE RUMINANT QUADRUPED CAMEL
    STORING POEMS IN YOUR HUMP
    A REAL CAPITALIST BANKING WORDS
LET'S SAY SOME BIG WORDS LIKE YOU LOVED TO DO
CARTOGRAPHY CHRONOLOGICAL GENERALISSIMO
    KISHA KISHA KISHA KISHA CYMBAL CYMBAL
      MESHUGANAH UTTER ARCHITECTONICS
HIGGLEDY-PIGGLEDY X-CHROMOSOME XEROGRAPHY

VAUDEVILLE-SOMERSAULTS IN MUTATIONAL
                                MEDITATIONS
A DELEGATION OF CRAWL-BARS COME TO VOTE
    SUPPRESSION AGGRESSION STARVATION
RAY, YOU GO THRU LITHOSPHERE TO LOCO
                                MOTIONING NIRVANA
PATRONYMIC MICROPHONIC PEDOMETER-EFFICACIOUS
    BE TISIPHONUS BE WAMPAUMPEAD
        QUERIMONIOUSLY QUERRELOUS
            QUICK TO JINGO JING A JINGO
BE BORN AGAIN A PERFECT BUTTERFLY
A BUDDHA FLITTING HIGH   FLYING HIGH
HA HA HA
                HA
            HA
                HA
                    HA
                        HA
                            HA
                                HA
                                    HA
                                        HA
                                            HA

RAY RAY YOU MADE IT
YOU HAD THE WORLD BY THE BALLS
SQUEEZED FOR ALL IT WAS WORTH
RAY BREMSER   SAINTLY

A Water Row Blues Bag

*— for Ray Bremser & Jeffrey Weinberg
at The Cherry Valley Arts Festival 8/8/98*

Say Ray Bremser
you were a real gone cat
at the Cherry Valley
Arts Festival
in the evening
as darkness
called out the Poetry Stars
with their Bag of Blues
to hang out
hooked on August
to be near Ginsberg's oasis
with evidence of Poetry
everywhere
compressed into three days
of Love
and old wonderments

Say Ray you told us
what happened
on road to Villacapampa
was it your Momma
your Poppa
your Sister
your Bonnie
who pointed with index finger
to unattainable Nirvana
in Mexico
to be with Señors
and Señoritas
in palatial cabanas
or maybe commune
with the ghosts
of Totonac runners
of Montezuma himself

or fantasize Uxmal
even bring back Trotsky
or dream Viva Zapata

Say Ray
what really happened
Ray
1000 pounds of ponder
blew you away
to wander across border
to wish away border guards
probation officers
judges
did you wash them out of mind
in a Rio Grande
river of beer

Say Ray
what happened
the day you filled
your bag of Blues
in Bordentown facility
and refilled in Trenton State
then off to riff thru the Holland
and Lincoln Tunnels
become Prince of Metropolitan
Poetry
and now 40 years later
still hovering
over Palisadian Heights
with your Jazz
for the New Millennium
with words to stick
between cracks
in America's Wailing Wall

Say Ray
what really happened
when you ticked-off
Society

with your Beat Shananigans
when you buried
once and forever
all the Grammarians
who stuck to the Rules
their Language decomposing
while you sang Ecstatic Blues
in Nova Broadcast
refilling your Water Row
Blues Bag
once again a biblical Conqueror

O say Ray Bremser
Scatman Celebrator
Jazz Daddy
physical body gone now
but not to be forgot
you painted the Moment
with heart
free born to be
Born Again
you be here now
on tape on page
always all ways
Born Again

1/28 – 2/2/99

Letter to Gregory

O Gargoyled friend
pondering centuries
in your storehouse
of horsedrawn chariots
recalling life
before daliesque womb-world
grecian urns trusting boys
loving masters trojan horses gods –

O gargoyled friend
stoned hypnotic
gazing into a grotesque
sculpted countenance
bequeathed imaginary breath
by ancient bards,
your atavistic mind
boglike screams
confined in muddy limbo –

do you cruise to nirvana
in your shiny
meta-developed wisdom
wondering sad gassed in nostalgia
for new york westside hiway
running with picasso detroit molochs
exhausting the young in haste,
or university cadenced minds
rapt in sheepskin dreams –

are you in delusion
spending gargoyle reveries of imagination
as incredulous insights
dropping poetic relatives
into whirlpool thoughts –

O gargoyled friend
sing self-effacing songs of love
trumpet poems
full of the joy of life
and blast the riot
from the mind
of our self-destructive
marathon civilization

Song for Gregory

There you be
the Serious Clown Prince of Poetry
singin' in the palace of a mountain king,
singin' your Royal Garden blues,
talkin' about throwin' out Death,
and Truth, and Beauty, out the window,
along with God, and Hope, and Charity,
and Faith, I'm sure.

That's some Serious Blues.
Even Saints'll go marchin' to that.
So tell me your dreams,
the funny ones that save day from nite,
your foamy Ballantine Valentines,
the mongo bongoed poppa-boppa-whoppers,
your ultimate odes to civilized bombs,
the money musk farewells to whiskey,
even the tipsy topsy-turvies
gasoline voodoo hoodoos,
the boogie woogie mindfield blues.
Hey, that's not misbehavin',
its just an old Indian song
asearchin' for Ulyssean deep-harbored treasure,
and singin a Bombay Blues.

What can anyone say?
"Everything's out the window?"
Just hold onto Humor?
That things just Are Illuminating Bliss,
Eternally Now?
And while I think of it,
"I'll keep an eye on my thoughts
are they mine or are they yours?"

CORSO

Gregory Corso: "There are poets
And there are people, both write,
But only poets can create"

He also said poets are romantics
O blessed poet O romantic child to the end
O runaway 19th century derivative poet
Drunk on dictionary
And brother poet Ginsberg's sunflower grown beautiful
In the big cittee's smog-scenes

O mischievous O drifter
O romantic croupier spinning your poems on the poetry wheel
While singing odes to Jersey toads in retrospect

O moonboy whose city lights mushroom bomb exploded
Over 60's U.S.A. altering death consciousness forever

O happy manipulator of saving grace in word-explosions on page
O poet celebrating Marriage & Police while thinking Power is a hat
O fabled flower of the beat generation did you love Fiorello
And wasn't Sacré Coeur the most beautiful church in the world
Did the gargoyles on Notre Dame outstare you meditating

O little-known remarkable editor of *Junge Amerikanishe Lyric*
    Anthology Germany 1960

O Herculean poetry heckler
Abrasive yet compassionate celebrating death while loving life
Was your 70 years nothing but romance
Knowing all could be a lie but marching
In Grecian cadence to discover ancient truth
And be in world-rhythm in your Gregorian chant
Your melodic rant

O fabled poetry reading interrupter as tinker-bell
Ringing up our conscience

O glorious disinvolver throwing out of the universe window
Judgmental concepts of Truth Pity and Beauty
And become mythic poetry-voice-reciter shaping personal history
As celebrator of the small life insights which are the real poetry
Seldom expressed

You a misanthrope was once said, but really an unbound lover
Seeking to give and receive love unconditionally

O seer knowing that life may be only a joke
A stance to take
As you became the serious clown-prince of poetry

Gregory Nunzio Corso March 26, 1930 – January 17, 2001

AMERICAN GURU

A.G.
Avant Garde
American Guru

AH

Poet is mid-century priest
Come thru the silence of the "ruling class."
Poet's essence celebrates life on this planet with compassion
Sums up wholeness from body parts
From within self
Expressed with ultimate sincerity
The wonder of self
Speaks and does with candor
Is poet-maker of particular truths
Rings freedom's bell with prophet-voice
He jumped off superstition like Columbus
He taught goodness as a naked mad scholar free fool
He snatched truth from society quicksand
And related the truth of trampled souls
Of minds disconnected from reality

A.G.
Avant Garde
American Guru

AH

Being son of mother who cared too deeply
And son of lyric-teacher-poet
Being brother uncle stepson lover cousin friend
Became hooked on the joy and the pain of language
His eyes focused kissing fame in the American night
His lips pronouncing truth while speaking sweet politics
And not so sweet too

A.G.
Avant Garde
American Guru

AH

Saw him heard him in cafes halls great universities
Confessing historical hysterical
Hair dishevelled Hassidic-bearded
Top of dome balded
Brain seeming to push thru skull 1960's
To burst upon world (a bomb of kindness)
his eyes analytical tender his universe

A.G.
Avant Garde
American Guru

AH

He saw all understood all
So energized went on and on and aum
An upstart expressor of giggly weed
A teacher and celebrator of gut feeling human
Insightful misunderstood
Scoffed at during this scuffling century
Because mind to mind goes so slowly
And his soul burnt with flesh in transit
With anxieties colored with hallucination

A.G.
Avant Garde
American Guru

AH

Overcome by filial therapy of old father time
He grappled and channelled his paranoia
Creeping as Yeats' creature second coming
To rendezvous Newark in Boulder in Michigan
A guru arrived at or going to Satori
Breathing harmonium-truths in holy chant
A high priest of ecstatic goof
Holding key to future in poet-hand

A.G.
Avant Garde
American Guru
Allen Ginsberg
6/3/26 — 4/5/97

AH

Lit. Kicks Summer Poetry Happening At The Bitter End

— for Brian Hassett, Levi Asher & David Amram

I see all the hip young people
think they've come to their bitter end
then in a summer's resurrection
rise to sing and dance
to prance the internet
to do the Lit Kick Lindy
let there be Beat Poets
and Jazz Magicians
let there be wailing Bleecker St solos
by poet-fools
to chase away their blues
to void their oiyz
to fill the world with good sonic vibrations
and pull all imaginable daisies
to place collect calls to the wild
and slam-dunk French ram-horn notes
to eternity
to kum kreate krank krush kronikle
krome yor soul
roll yor stone bone yor mole
yor holy hairy hole
be a haiku in alkor disguize
kum howl yor squint
trowel yor skin yor skink
yor super ding-ding
mock yor kock
yor tick-tock-klock
yor mitey klunk
bridge the fridge
the ridge the memory store
the traffic gore the Wall St Dow
the klack and klink
go kut some slack

quack quack quack quack quack
be neat flirt with the beat
beat yor meat never retreat
go go spank the klank
shoot the shoot
shoe the moon
the heavenly goon
and sing this krazy toon
don't shun the fun
or smoke the bun
or hipe the pipe
this great summer nite
free-verse yor nurse
but stay outta her purse
do yuuhh muse
don't kook yor goose
but goose the kook
with a starry starry glee
be so jazzy jazzy kool
and go go go go go
be be be be be be
all you kan be
beeee

7/21/99

I Got a Right to Sing the Blues

— for Laura

Every time the phone rings "call waiting"
I think it's you calling one last time

Forty-two years just a drop in the bucket
I got a right to sing the blues

I don't get along very well without you
I find myself making one wish too many

This year the weather inside is stormy
I got a right to sing the blues

The drawers in your dresser are empty
Hangers in your closet are bare

There's no reflection in your mirror
I got a right to sing the blues

When it's time to say good-nite
And I feel myself talking to empty space
And there's only one pillow on a double bed
I got a right to sing the blues.

PEARL

— for Flo

Be a lite and know love
                    simply finger it

Build a saint in your vision
                    but don't glide thru life in reverse.

Have your God hide your drink
                    for a rainy day.

Know your illusions are genuine
                    and nothing but dreams.

Know your love lives on the planet
                    and is lost on the internet.

Stretch imagination in your mirror
                    and dance with it.

In dreams cast yourself
                    as a pearl.

And be ready to wail
                    like John Coltrane.

Lift-Off

Lift-Off 1

I lift you off the page
put a fix on you
        sic
           pic
              yoo-hoo
ditto wham! Ooh you fix the 'n'
where the 'j' should be
and all being 'in' or 'out'
              poem-times
creating hell with ease
I call for pie
      and risk category
yes, poets dressed positively in blue orgons
become O.K. mysteries
           misery's
              less friends
konged
   disturbed in their ego-eggs
el niño tingles
tangled with guys hiding poems from you
just ask them to suck & titi
late at nite
or to couple on diction airy
to farm words
to raise high their drools
to hide their poems in gene pools
to yoshi everywhere
and aik shang shine sing oot
to be good and cut out to prove
let there be free rants
           rents
              parking meter events
let there be high thighs
        and skinny sighs
           be cool

let's note this down while
listening to Dizzie
and surf the net dot-comming all way to a spiderland
I be rare and beat yoo-hooing to heaven
I hear visionary aural trumpets and sax-flipping
so old friends note this in your audio cassettes
and shoulder your suffery odes noteworthy this nite
amen

Lift-Off 3

i decide   i'm done
                begin to whistle
E   then   if i can crank up
        and
kill the AND in me
                mew   AND   mean nothing
short of dialogue a tool tewt
geo-babbling   kibbling   dribbling
in dementia   as if dribbles are drifting
metaphors to harpoon with
i decide i'm not nearly done
                            i must
be a lout –
do inY I O jelly this is
Nothing   but a life of mistakes
                            i miss
babbling but the thing that
                        kept up
the illusion the done deal
                        or a million
deals and dont's
            i think was his name
MICHAEL   in double jeopardy
            as if
super imposed to form a bond between meese
and hip cats
        a giving
                Thous & i
both   me and BLY and by   blither & wither
but why   and Pavlov   drinking Pepsi
dice thrown   wrong number   nothing in it
except a jingle or two   appearance is ALL
oops   pardon my ilk   my squeek   my teeth
set tite in misfortune   there is only
HOPE   the "Spirit" transforms   the white
bread to toast   is jazzy   sling

entering off a Feeling   pole has nothing
to do with jealousy   just pull the strings
regret nothing   do not hesitate
office jingles with fast umbrellas
its all this is   a test   alkaline
at random   lets fit all this together
knead it   with poets of another millennium
poets who fold dactyls into napkins
                                    as Dins more
did   rite tidings   uttered in code to –
gather our national D N A deliberately
HA   as usual   a pot Control
                              op scene
i decide i've had enough
                              my position is
contraried this October
                        that leaves trees
baring   with no bearing   or near to Hawaii
go for it today
                  drop your prose
                              play the game
                                    mask it
take your chance with a Boardwalk pass
go all out aboard
                        a trip to December
its all on paper
                  drink Pepsi and see
you can stop a star
                        it is   or it ain't
          or
cain't re-establish a protein con versation
sayonara   oobli doo
SO   it all mounts to heightened awareness
just take me   never forsake me
              (jas k tak Me
tagalong manli ah PoP poor peep ah rooney)

Lift-Off 4
Neutral

I reek neutrality
trek weeks whippy
dine on media & meditate
me & Pollie McKirk sit on a keg
go thru the nite hot on coffee
brains liberated yay Love
Illusion lit ess picked up on
O long in Cool lonely on the edge
I peer laf naw a lifer even
yes has hash ho in urgham
oop of course a seal hurds me
O mess of fovvidaaa
a joust outside de hospital
1/2 a gram mother in dew
some sort of hula a hustle
I sit hunchbacked on teak
IS THIS OSAKA it toomee
I forge a dow in and deer soy
Orion in the nite no way
I pulse dowd or gemdow
gimme blues gimme titilation relations
you con
you know how dow mundo condo
undecided no
a seminar miracle non tidy
tracking is a mainman's line
you so of a bitch
your nose is a duplicate
made of poor paper
a poor pop work of humanity
you okay dude
until another author comes along
that's so irrational
set in iron

a divine message hear
you know what I'm sayin?
its yin yankd over yeowl meow
wilco & toads with klieg & jewels
& lands in dirt is thankful
in rennet Om times Om
writes on the mall
vivacarious
a bag to steal like bagatell
my chair in the university comes alive
where angels fear to tread
retreads for the payoff
which comes afterward
its an experience dexperdeing
a rough inknote a mishagosh
forsaken
shaken diddly doo

Lift-Off 7
Abracadabra

I'll open with disses and dosses and stresses kisses
I'll open   open   open   open
Sess-a-me   sess-a-me
Mucho
Abracadabra
I'll get up   or I won't
I do
With insistence
With a flourish
A Royal Flush
A dissassembling that which was
A part of me
But no resemblance now
I hope
I'm a waffler
So I do or do I don't
I do
My dreamscope emerges
I'm loco in motion
Unzippering my real world
Full of Emotion
I mean to be inspired
I'll pin a bow
A ribbon of good wishes
On the world
I'll be brite and happy
Sunnyside up

Lift-Off 8
I'm A Serious Dealer

It's Friday
I'll get up on life's deck
To a Royal Flush
Or I won't
But I do
Full of free farcical interferences
Later I come up subway steps
To see a sea of AIDS simmering in city
The next move is up to me

I almost peed on the train
What choice do I have
color it insistent
Filled with World Anxiety
World gone loco in zippered movements

I dreamt dissassembled
Shuffling life's deck of jokers
I'm a Serious Dealer
I'll get up to a Royal Flush
Or I won't,
I do

I say to you's
You are all Superdicktionary
Teetering on the brink
Do as I do
Or don't
But do answer my buzz
This time I'll reach my hang-out
I'll recognize symptomaniac judgments
I'll k nock   k nock   k nock   k nock
K nock at the millennium door
An urge
A heavy duty itch for heaven

Lift-Off 9

Flying Tambourine Klop In The Tonic

— *for Suzie Ibarra, Charles Burnham & Cooper Moore*

SAY HEY THIS THING ISN'T A RITE
ET TU DO ME THEN SO
OH HOW TIS HOW IS IT HEVVY STUFF THIS FIRST SET
SO AM SO KLOPPED IN SHOCK DOWN IN HEAP
ME WITH A KISS FOR EVRY ONE KLOPPED IN HEAD
ITS GOSPEL THIS PM I AM ONLY A BOY
WITH A BEAT BEAT I SAY NOW LIKE WOW
IT AR YEW SIS BRO IT MUSS BE JAH AFTER ALL
AFTER ME AS I FOLD AND WANDER KLOPPED
WITH FLYING TAMBOURINE
OH STEVE BE RITE MY ANGEL I AM SHOOK IN SHOCK
GUIDE ME OH MA MA MA RESCUE ME I AM SO IN NEED
OH BLOODY GOSPEL SUCH A SURPRISE
IT IS YIN YANG MAYHEM
MAYBE STROKED SHOCK TO HEAD WHAT A SCENE
SUE SEE AND BURN AM AM I & A COOPER
AND IN TONIC I AM POMMED
ME WHO BE A JAZZ SEE POET IT BE ME GOLLEE
GOIN DOWN TO BE MOORED TO DECK
IN NEW YORK TIMES
GONE DOWN JUST ONE OF THOSE NITES TO GAIN PASSAGE
IS THIS MY THING O FUN NITE TURNED AROUND
O HOO I AM KIND OF UH NO DINERO
AM KIND OF SURREAL CLIMB UP BABBLEE LADDER
TO HEAVEN GATE A GOSPEL TONIC
A LIFE OF MIXED TIMES
IN AND OUT THE DOOR NO TICKEE YES BLOODEE SHIRTEE
A MUSIC LAD IN A FOOL PHASE OF AM I
PLACE MY SHOOTING-STAR HEAD EYES MY POET'S TOOLS
AND GROWING EGG QUARTER INCH ABOVE ON FOREHEAD
THIS COULD BE MY LOSS OF POWER OVER WORDS
OR SUCCOR OUT OF IT MY WITNESS HOVERS OVER
NY CITY DESK TIMES GOOD THERE'S NO BOLT ON DOOR

I SEE WIPING BLOOD AS I LEAVE AFTER SECOND SET
AND DROP BLOODY TOWEL MIXED WITH MELTED
ICECUBES
AND I STAND TALL MAKE NO WAVES REACH OUT
WITH LOVE AND CD GIFT WITH SAX & PERCUSSIVE
VITAMINS   O DIDDLY I DOO I AM TOO KINDLY
GINSBERG SAID 40 YEARS AGO I SIT FOR SHORT TIME
ON THAT THAT THIS WAS NOT A RITE OR RIGHT
THERE SHOULDA BEEN AN SOS TIS HOW I SEE IT NOW
SO IT IS SO IT IS STEAL THIS WOO THIS IS

Lift-Off 10
Om Dot.Com

— for Mark Sonnenfeld

NITE FILLS ME
        A MUSE OF 'N LITE 'N MEANT
  THAT WHICH IS
       APPEARS TO BE
THAT WHICH IS VIVID
   MY SEARCHING FACE
FLUID AND CELLULAR
   A TOON OM DOT A MARK
COPYRITE DOT COM
FINGERS TO LIPS TO EARS
I SEE NO EVIL IN
OR COME OUT OF FILAMENT
OUT OF BURSTING NEURO MOMENT
       move meant plurissimo holy om's
A BOM-BOOM BOO BURSTING IN NATION ALL IT
I LOVE IT   CANNOT LEAVE IT
MEMORY REMAINS   VOID
THIS IS AT ONCE SALTY A DOG OM COM DOTTING
EGGS AND EGO BEATEN TO BEATIFICATION
the deal is rigged for the new millennium
AN OM IN US ERA ALL FOR RENT
STOCK HEADS TO WOO WOO SHRED DREAMS
I AM CAUGHT IN OWN GREED-OM-NET I CALL
SOUNDS OF CRASHING SEE
HEAR WAVES WAILING SEND HIGH ROLL MESSAGE
O HOLY   HOLY   HOLY
O HOLY   OM DOT COM   DIDDLY I RECKON
SEE I LIST 'N SEA
HOLDING SHELL OF SELF OM EAR
A CONFERENCE OF I-TOLD-YOU-SO's
      SALE OF SOULS
O LATER MAN THE BOWERY BECKONS
   GRIEF

ALL HALLOWED
YET HOLLOW
I ALLOW UP TO NO GOOD I SAY
                         HORSERADISH
I CRY
    INCREMENTS
          OF OM NISH ENCE
EATS ONE'S APRIL RISING A RISKY BUSINESS
A TEXAN OM BRAY   EXCUSE ME GOV'NOR
EVEN 100 or more million
I MAGINE LONG HORN OM NIVORES
       RIDE
HEARD AMERICAN HIWAY
       POOR
EXCUSES LATE NITE
          SHOW ME YOUR COMPASSION
HUNGRY IMAGES GONE BERERK IN COMPUTERLAND
OLD STORY ONE CANNOT EAT GOLDEN MACHINERY
    DREAMING VIRTUAL McDONALD'S DOUBLE BURGER
THE MEAT OF MOMENT SHOULD BE UPWARD MOVE MEANT
LIKE OTHERS I WANT TO TAKE MY TURN
HOLD HEALTHY FLESH IN MY HANDS
GO ON OM A TE UM CONJUGAL FANTASY
IT IS ALL SO DARN DOT COM KOOL
I CONJUGATE   DO IT LATIN
OMPHALLIC MEANDERING
RESOLVE SOLVE SOUL U BO KNEE BEND
          OMMING
MIST OF MIST   DOUBT DISS-SOLVING
SEEN IN REVOLVING MIRROR
MIRROR MIRROR MIRROR ON OMMINGWALL
          ?
OMMINGWALL WALL WAILS MESSAGE
DISS SOLVING REVOLVING
MASSAGE IN CRACKS
GOD ETERNAL READS OM NIP O TENT
          MAY BE
ON HIS/HER INTER GALACTIC NET WEB
ROAM KARMIC HIWAY

                    GO
                        OM
                            SPREE
HEY NEAL CASSADY
        ALL SPOILS BELONG YA YA SEE
OM BUDS MAN   DRINK SUDS
HEAVEN FOAMS   SING SING
SING GOOD MAN
            CLARINET KING OF OM
SOLVE MYSTERIOUS CYBER MISSING SPACE
a load that's a
        THERES A NEW CENTURY
A TIME MACHINE YEARNING TO BE FREE
INFINITE FINGERING RIDE COM PUTER HIWAY
OMMING   OM MING   OMMING   OM MING
TO SATORI DOT COM OM *VIRTUAL NIRVANA*

Lift-Off 12
Dolphinity

— for Piero Heliczer

S O S   O Sad
        please
keep me on
i'm subsceptically yours
       yoo hoo
I am mad hooing for you
just think
go knee-up with me
i keep up or tried to with you
    in Amsterdam   then France
i hugged you on the telefone
    loved your chutzpah
i do   did   love your impishness
if you think its neccessary to do so
i'll dedicate this to you
your silky simple sample Delancey poetry
    you shared in the late fifties
        early sixties in the Ikon bookstore
you stormed around in your amazing
    leather boots, your small frame
a picture of hipness
       with invisible lanyard
    'twas weird   dont you think
dont you think its weird
    dont you think
there may be a relationship
to tipe it sub sceptically
    with
tipoze   typoze   typose   to tipe to
    poze
to be sub standard speller
    P P
poor not only a liquid poze
    we are all letters

to whom
                WAS I SAYIN OR
AM i sayin anything
                is there some agency involved
i do see but i c
        a letter
i do see i am s-p-a-c-e-d
                out
                        all over this page
                                you can read
into this as man facturing of
        off
course
    who over sees
            is there an agency
i read into things
        spaced
            the course
C depicts all i see
            never-the-less
a 3-combo word skirts the issue
                        issues
a spinning den
        69 combi nations if
THERE'S AN EMERGENCY INVOLVED emerging
                i see but like i said c is a letter
only later man
    the pajamas are in the mail
den a man can rot in lop
                in short
recyle
    under wear
        in houseboat
in canal Amsterdam
            recall St Marks
poetry Pot
        so SAD to see you gone
hardly a word said
            so SAD
            so mad
some said a dactyllic pree historic Poetry Monster

mister H,
        on your bike
                    tripping across
Europe REAL
            ah each moan socks it to me
i'm blabbing
        babbling and teering
                my
rolling nerves   and rockin stuff
                bummers
bashful you weren't
            there can't be any
retaliation now
            you're a gone guy
                    BEAT
i believe
avoiding koko angry pew
                do
or dont know the Real to reel in words
make them come in from outer space
make me feel   lose my table manners i
            scat in C-attle
                with piano and clarinet
i gnu   mean   think of you in silk
                a wren
s-t-r-e-t-c-h-i-n-g your lines
                        a comic strip
literal ness
        take back seat
                high as
a brother theo
            green as a sic ticking
tacked toes
        tickling thoughts of biting
the bullet
        in a sense
                o take me before
a general court marshal
    i seem to be in sum in a kind of trouble
                commas

are coming
        thunder is clapping lurid
pounds of ms pounds   pounds pounding
in head
    Italian tales of ezra
                pounding
while you were there
                there's no rational
answer to your tale
                O Sad Piero
dead on Europa bike
                years after nazis
killed your father
                attention   attention
attention   attention
                those were the years
loose   national brains   gone berserk
overflowed borders
                how did you get to
Amsterdam anyway,
                becum Beat,
                        yes i
can see that
        sad memories
                attachments
                        broken
sad trumpet playing taps   while
grouchy sax played down the s-t-r-e-t-c-h
                                O Sad Piero
                post mod fate slain
on his Poet-cycle
                cant say any more
or babble on   ahem   ahem
                world full
of hackles
        god bless his holy word
and photo-images
                his stint on earth be done
i under stand under state   stand talking
                this
in grief   a Real Son of Poetry

Lift-Off 15
Get Your Haiku On Rte 66

already gone 1000 miles
miles and miles to go
american landscape nibbling
read incredible billboards NATIONAL NEWS
PONDER POOR SWEET WHITMAN BALLAD-OF-AMERICA
wondering wandering bald roads
boldly hurtling thru hypnotic nite
rough American shoulders
where only mightiest flora grow

     on rte 66
     city dust smog
     automobile speeds
     hot tires separate

west coast beckons
Gaté gaté parasamgaté et mingus
in traffic miles to go
odd smoke e um mire
ad c.o.d.'s G.O.D.'s S.U.V's
utilities futilities in honor of
2 cees 2 esses is it necessary
keep my I in this diction airy
my ear in toon with my soul
minty slopes rip mountains
miles to go
I adorn nite begin again
in the sockets national headline glare
say what so yet est gaze
sad midnite moody mercado on wheels

     reach thru hole in hiway sad
     noon moans misery
     Janis Joplin singing
     O Lord Mercedes Benz
     YES

Lift-Off 16
Watchman In The 99¢ Store

MAN ON LADDER inside store doorway
"Leave all bags at the counter!"
Hey, I only want some envelopes and oregano.
I wanna sing glissando about this day.
Whaddya think's in my bag,
a puff or two?

O I see, it's that Beat Seer
musta passed this way on his scooter!
I wanna violate the rules,
that's MY BAG initialed with ACLU
I keep my eyes on things that matter
I stretch space
and go on the yellow brick road
FREE
to shun the Errors 'cause I drink
The Milk Of Kindness
& I wanna share it with all on Broadway
I'm still dialing The Tao
dealing with outrageous #'s
and staring at the bargains
in the 99¢ store
lite bulbs garlic salt 99¢ brooms
sunlite dishtergent steel wool
Hey Neighbor! Lookie lookie
I want that man on the ladder for 99¢

TRUST ME MAN!
I am stirred to ecstasy I tell you
all the THINGS!
THIS STORY IS A LIFT-OFF
I'm in the 99¢ store
I don't even think in this case
there's a key ring to this

A MAN SITTING ON A LADDER NEAR THE DOOR
IS WATCHING ME!
What kinda thing goes on here?
Business is based on Trust

Yes the luck of it is Honesty
and now the angst of a clown on a ladder
lo lo lo a hell of a maneuver
a clown up on a ladder a real Downer
I say GET Real
get off your greedy ass
get off your goolie by golly
with your howitzer eyes cocked on me
tin pan reflections of the Real
HEY THERE'S A MAN ON A LADDER
NEAR THE DOOR OF THE STORE

He's watching me for his 99¢ worth
Woolworth never did this!
My temperature is rising
A chance of showers tonite
I spot a 99¢ umbrella
OK I feel like a shoplifter
I'm barely done with my green tea high
Can you imagine a guy on a ladder
near the door of his store
A M A Z I N G I tell you

I'm teed off
I need some KAVA KAVA
I must get rid of this Image
A MAN ON A LADDER NEAR THE DOOR
OF HIS STORE
O OM OM OM OM OM

Business is Trust
I am stirred in my need
CONFUSED
WHAT DID I NEED HERE ANYWAY?

Lift-Off 21
Tokyo Stroll

— for J.G., T.M., H.W.,
Y.K., Y.O. & S.D.

I am sad and Tokyo Blue
I dreamt a mil yen haiku
And grew delirious with desire
My alpha beating with masked intentions
Legs cramped
Eternal universe wearing a phony face
Hysterical mind holding exorbitive premonitions
O Buddha invested with crazy wisdom
O Lord a loco weed grows in my soul
I take out of the chaos
a blank crash insurance document
Think to slay the fearful airplane dragon
who wears yankee baseball cap
Dig it my own om in us all
My racial memory
is as permanent as sand castle
This said with ear to seashell
As I stroll amazing Tokyo
An amazing Tokyo blue newsday
A dream
I must call halfway around world
My Zen heart beats in New Jersey
And my voice is lost
With AT & T direct-call card
O I am lost on Kioi-cho chi Yoda-ku
I must seek Yusuke Keida in Sanjo-shi
in his Blue Beat Jacket
I scream for him in holy silence

Help me at this crossroad
I am lost in Narshi mire marsh-moment
I've gon meshuggee

seeking impossible applause
Love hung up to dry out desire
Hooked on Printed Matter
Lines cast to me by Taylor Mignon and Hillel Wright
Attractive Yaponesia bait
I am sad strolling Tokyo Blue
Spooked and helpless in doom-dream
Blue black sky surreal
A Dada-Zenist a Zen-Dadaist
Snacking Yakitori-yo yo ma
No frill oodles of noodles
on Rappongi near the crossing
I stroll with treasured desires unfulfilled
Kazuko Shiraishi's voice in memory
I am strolling Tokyo Blue a No-show Poet
Am not really inTokyo
Confused by crowded subway rumors
Crushed by Reality
and fear of Sarin gas
I stroll in mind
to resolve this in a dream
Negative thoughts go around masked
Ego goofing with paranoid visions
Awareness heightened
Incredulous A-bomb continues exploding in dream
as if it is real   it was
Conscience troubled
Recurring recurring recurring recurring
Unbelievable images recurring recurring recurring
NAGASAKI   HIROSHIMA
Yap   yap   Yaponesia

THIS IS NO GOOF
I seek solace in Tanaka Temple Town
Poemetry translations of guilt
Overbearing as I am lost on Tokyo streets
My spirit seeks Tokyo forgiveness
I hang out in a Japanese urban jungle
Seek escape in Make-believe
I am a Sumo

wrestling loneliness and guilt
Go to Akusawa to meditate long-distance
As I run from John Gribble on phone
at American Tenple University
And run from Shoichi Fuji of Saitama
young Japnanese friend I am fearful of
maybe C.I.A. with his calligraphic intentions
All seems statistical political oriental
in dream in imaginary Tokyo stroll
blue paranoia heightened awareness

Unneccessary quandary I'm in
Some poet-pal I am
Duplicitous
Realize karmic dragon I fear
is myself
Breathing fire-thoughts in foreign dream
Knowing I am nothing but wizened toad
croaking cramped poems
Tokyo-wishing to sip zen tea
in ceremonial rock garden
A Whitman wild son of Father Woe
veering trancelike translucent thru Shinjuko
drunk on sake
urinating against Kabuki-cho wall
squatting over hole in ground
bathing in another's bath water

What am I doing
listening to gongs to gongs to gongs
going off in my reverberating weepy mind
I stroll Blue Tokyo with unfulfilled desires
Stroll toward ghostly hostess bar in Ginza
neon hypnotic overwhelmed by price of life
in Shinjuko's Kabuki-cho district
I am zen-bopped with Geisha-visions
seek gentle soft-spoke woman
to understand me love me
with quiet Japanese words in ear
and soft hands to carress me

as I read Blue Poems to her
Prosoke gongs to ring in ear
eternal music of universe
to drown my unforgettable croaking
to drown mad sad damn cadenza only in dream
Stroll Blue Tokyo with misplaced spaced intentions
Built-up recitations of I want
hung heavy in unholy desire
Must meditate dig Illumination
in the silence of Hama Rikyu Garden
Must avoid Tokyo Desires
or end up a crazy Poet-cat
scatting words that hiss
like licking honey off sharp knife-edge

And I wake up thinking of Yuko Otomo
in her mother's Sasabo garden
planting Spring's first haiku
to review in Asahi News
All   Will   Be   Well

Lift-Off 23
TV Mute Ant in Candystore

Sit at counter near pinball   watch play
Bare bark dig mute raisins march on screen
Pinball raises bark march ping skit
Poeticians march mute march March
M P candystore energy galaxy swat
Mute cows plop plop slip sip and moo
Dig poeticians mute portray past green church
Candystore magnifies drive suite sweetly
Counter praises raise energy swat build bank
Messenger with wires raises hackles
Hacks ten and lies
Monkeys split energy slip cows
Pinball pings offer march to suite
Raisin bread magnifies poetry swat
Poeticians dig mute supposition

Candystore skitters
Dig #1 California raisin mute bond
McRaisin mute slips in counter march
NBC Saturday plays globe theatre
Cold drinks on brink of black out
Blame mute poetry hackling monkey shines
Eye blinks counter to energy

Yankee is to blame resets raisin
Horse called macaroni disguises monkey
Mute ping magnifies pinball
Candystore is the medium
The massage is the medium
Message is the massage
Message is mute in a monkeys beard
Wires hackle   cows mute
Got milk
Bread rises the price of a counter
Raisins march with mute poeticians
Mute counters mute ant in candystore

Lift-Off 24
LETTER TO BOB

WOW BOB, WHAT A RIFF
LOBBED ME A POEM, MAN,
YOU STUCK WEBSTER IN HIS DICTION AIRY,
AND QUITE THE CONTRARY OF WHIM
YOU GOT GERT RUDE ZOUNDING LIKE
SHE RUBBED HER QUEENIE GENIE
AND CAME UP ITZ A CASSIO SCAT TO FELLATIO
ROCKING & ROLLING SMOKING MARY'S
WHILE SQUINTIN AT CLINTON
I'M THINKIN WHOOPS!
IN THIS NEW YORK GOLD BURG
AVOIDIN THE WEST NILE SKEETER SPRAYBUCKS
PLAYIN GOD BLESS AMERICA
THIS LAND OF LIVE VERY
ALL FOR ONE
AND ONE FOR ALL WHO FALL INTO BURRITOS
FULL OF HOT SALSA LUV COME SOON
KINDA MAKES OL BUDDHA
WISH HE WERE A TEX-MEX
SITTING IN A CAFE 2ND AVE
INSTEAD OF LICKING OLD ZEN-FINGERS
THERE IS A PERFECT NOTION
IN THIS IMPERFECT NATION
SAY SOME SENSIBLY IT IS JUST IS JUST
IS THAT JUST JUST
THINKIN UNIVERSAL THINKING
A STICK UP THE ASS IN MAD MANHATTAN
CITY OF SHAFTS AND SHIFT STICKS
LIKE STICK AN ARREST IN THE PIE
AND PULL OUT A PLUNGER
O NO TEARS NO SIGHS JUST LIES
A WHOLE MAN WRITES OF RITES
AND TRIES AND TRIES
AND TEARS INTO IT TWISTS
AND TIES UP HIS WORDS

SMOOTH LIKE MAYOR NAISE
KOOLS BYE AND BYES
ADDRESSES THE 2ND ADDRESS
LOST AT FIRST IN AN INK-STAMPEDE
LOOKED TO BE ATE BY POSTMAN
O THOSE GUYS POST INSANITIES
DELIVER THE GOODS TWICE ALRIGHT
TO GET IT RIGHT
THAT'S NICE
CROSS MY HEART
IT'S A WONDER WHY
THE WEIGHT OF A CRATE OF JUNK MAIL
CAN CRASH THE STARTING-GATE
O gaté gaté gaté parasamgaté
GO ALL THE WAY THRU 3 ZONES
LIKE THAT FRENCH RAMBO GUY
WHO STAMPED THIS MYSTERY
STUCK IT INTO AN ANCIENT VELOPE
MUSTA BEEN VERY VERY TICKLED
THIS CON VERSE ZEN SATION COMES AND GOES
RAMBLING WITH CHOICE WORDS GAMBLING
TICKLE & TACKLE & TOCKEE TOCKEE
AFORE SAID LIKE TELL IT LIKE IT IS
HUH, SEE, ITS ALL ABOUT FROGGY
I NO EAT YOUR LEGS, UGH, LEGS
MAYBE GO JERK LIKE THAT CAD-A-LACK
CATALOGUE PERFORMANCE GRANVILLE UNDER BRIDGE
WHATEVER ELSE THE RATS DID TO HIM
THEY DID LEAVE HIM HIS CAMELS
TO RIDE TO GRAVE ON ITS SAID
WITH WHOLE LOT OF SNIDE
NOT TO BE SOLD IN BARNS OR NOBLE TO SPEAK
OR CHECK OUT MAD COWS & BROKEN MEAT
NEATLY CUT UP AMERICAN LANGUAGE LIKE THIS
BARKING & CHATTERING LIKE A MONKEY
WITH THIS NEW YORK CAT
HEY, ITS CRAZY MAN,   CRAZY MAN

Lift-Off 27
Poem Made Out Of Whole Cloth

GAB OR DINE
ON WORDS
WOVEN
OUT OF WHOLE CLOTH
TO SHINE
LIKE SPACECRAFT TAKE-OFF
GRAB ONE
BY SEAT
OF
PANTS

Lift-Off 28
RECKONING

RUNS   DOWN   PLASTIC LEGS
    TOTALLY
        UNLIMITED MEALS
   SOFTLY TEEMS OF YEARZ
    YEYZ
to have have not or space in hab it
   encomium THEMED THEREIN VITA MIN
TIN THESIS MEMBER SHIP BLACK MAGIC
   WILD HAY SOWN sure memory
  alto leaps over void
OLD NULL-SKULL LABEL LEASHED
    ME BEAST
TABLE SETTLED HUFFFS DOLK
    PUFFS AWARD-WORLD
  ON   BACK COVER
LOLLY POPS LOTS POISE
    SPRAY SPRAY NAY
POUT SMIT-IN-POET PORT SNORT
      FROZEN bits
   OOH WAT LUCK RAIN
    MEMBERSHIP IS TEAM
    ONE STORY
  NO LUCK HUNG
THER AMEN A GRAM TOO MUCH
  SEE   HOVERING
HOVERINGS HOOVER
   HOWEVER ON THE face of IT
    STORY LIFT-OFFS
  ITS TOO MUCH   TOO SPIRITUAL
  ONE NEVER KNOWS
    ITS SPIRITUAL
THE THEIR MOM—EATER $_RIS^ES$

        with luck

the U.S. buried in correct churchyard
a new century city video
GRAPHIC A NON
and a lark
duos separate
pan a vision
creech and crong
crang push pins thru berserk posters
posture sappling dappled in the Apple
tin hay hey wild like like
reckoned
pushed thru needy eyes
spirits s$_o$$_w$$_n$

d
o
w
n   spastic

O LEGS OF ME HEART
HAND CLAPS
SLAP SLAP SLAP SLAP
c a p s wave waver except
party vis A vision
Green card de puss fits
100 watts in a name

O Future make change
5¢ bottle of paris
O watts in a Future
or on the plain
its aar yut foan
me red and Hol sum
like NOSTOC a Goal
to score ah oud odd eye dr.
There its said
once locked out
after gradation of events
a graduation dance
wrested
heart pumping

jumping steep thru century's
    STARLESS STORIES
DOWN
      S_TA_IR_S
D_OW_N stairs
      on nape of neck
what wonders beyond reach of reckoning
wretched cherry-pick-come
    make no mistake
tree seen sawn memory
    futile sewn eternally
      change make plainly

argh jut foam
    again form a red hol sum
    a hol man nostalgic
    Massachusetts Nostoc awardee
      words to lift-off
    out of encomium thesis
      there all odds dance outside

lock-out the sky pump wet minds
with pints of mall
    Washington beckons
all comes down every year
lacy omelets
    the US in a lite churchyard
      video classic
parsed territorial anger in Florida
      'round midnite
      with
graphic a non lack-eye vision
    deal on bin swass
      all down
    imaginary ragas sing wasted
      beckon bad luck reckoned
    TIME IS A MEMBERSHIP IN THE SPIRIT

Lift-Off 29

— for Gregory Corso

you loaned me your romantic eye
and I was so worried
  read this
    it was a great time
time of Beat on page
      in heart
before the dot coms and moog melts
when we all wore felt hats and
slouched by the hour
    hanging our screws
loose ordinary to shoot up down
America's hi-ways
     to course thru
displaced city veins
     inevitably house-laden
loaded on Bols blackberry poem-accompaniment
where composed whirly eyes worried
lead to inevitable excellent sex free baby
creative Pepsi generation cum loud
      cum out cage
generate personality conflict as
generations engage in social security war
each wanting twice as much to gamble
hey baby if that's whats to be
   then
an eye for an eye
    one knows all is
going down tell a gram fill li po lit ticks
fame and fortune wearies me
I feel totally blue
    a dreamy lad
dissolved in the 90's
     how did i live this long
slugged my pox fate inflated with knees
gone shaky eyes bammed from above I thought

I desired more than most
                    positively Poetry
heroic in poedinum drumming
poems on the spot
              on the pot
                     om dot insipid
slipped into performance
                  O loan me your
conscience
        your confidence
                    or mock me
with your Keatsian balls
              I'm only a lad
a lost guru on a patterned roll
seedy ears and eyes voice influenced
        by hype
and typed measly do's in a jam
zithery withery no bam left by hype
    O that's so grand
        I'm not so but
              Gregory Corso is
              grand
respectfully beat and installed in the woe
          of his story
    O I'm goin' to be marvelously senile
on all my roads this list is lusty till now
half hid had run off the page lifted off own
                        dick sh un wary

This book has been made possible with generous support from the following organizations and people:

Water Row Books
Long Shot Productions
Elaine & Norman Teitcher
Jonathan Teitcher
Arielle Teitcher
Jack & Terri Silverman
Laura Silverman
Peter & Helene Bence
Marshall Brooks
Carol Chosid &
    Richard Richiuso
Dave Church
Andy Clausen
Steve Dalachinsky
Paul Drexel
Laurie Feinberg
Marty and Marla Genee
Ralph Gonzalez &
    Suzanne Poor
Steven Hartman
Bob Holman
Eliot Katz & Vivian Demuth
Arthur Konigsberg
Rozanne Levine &
    Mark Whitecage
Joel Lewis

Tsaurah Litzky
Jonathan & Maureen London
Nancy Mercado
Tom Obrzut
Yuko Otomo
Eve Packer
Alan Pizzarelli
David Plakke
Gene D. Plumber
Pola, Jill & Marjorie Rapaport
Michael Reardon
Mr & Mrs George Resetar
Perry Robinson
David Roskos
Geri Roth
Ron Rusnak
Hal Sirowitz
Danny, Caroline,
    Casey & Levi Shot
Rose & Harry Tuvel
Cor van den Heuvel
Janine Pommy Vega
Joe Weil
Jeffrey Weinberg
Flo Wetzel
Marshall Wise

Herschel Silverman is a longtime contributor to scores of literary magazines including: *Long Shot, Talisman, Blue Beat Jacket, Connections, Butcher Block,* and *The Home Planet News.* He has been a New Jersey State Council on the Arts Fellow in Poetry, and served as Guest Editor of *Long Shot #17, It's The Jews!* Herschel has been anthologized in the 70th anniversary edition of *The Pavan* at St. Peter's College, *Bluestones & Salt Hay* (Rutgers University Press) the first comprehensive anthology of NJ poets in over 50 years, and *The Outlaw Bible of American Poetry* (Thunder's Mouth).

He is the inspiration and subject of Jonathan London's *The Candystore Man,* a children's book based on Mr. Silverman's thirty-four years as owner operator of Hersch's Beehive in Bayonne, New Jersey. In 1998, he was designated the Inaugural Poet at the swearing in of Mayor Joseph V. Doria Jr and the Municipal Council of Bayonne. A beloved and much respected poet, Herschel has been a catalyst in encouraging younger poets in their work. Mr Silverman is a United States Navy veteran of both the Second World War and the Korean Conflict. He is the father of two children; Elaine Teitcher and Jack Silverman, and three grandchildren.